Japanese: The Spoken Language in Japanese Life

By Osamu Mizutani
Translated by Janet Ashby

The Japan Times, Ltd.

ISBN4-7890-0161-X

Copyright © 1981 by Osamu Mizutani
Translated by Janet Ashby
Jacket design by Detake Koji

First edition: December 1981
Second printing: October 1982

All rights reserved. No part of this book may be reproduced in any form without the permission of The Japan Times, Ltd.

Original Japanese language edition "Nihongo-no Seitai" published by Sotakusha Inc., 3-12, Misakicho 1-chome, Chiyoda-ku, Tokyo 101, Telephone: 03-291-6841.
Copyright © 1979 by Sotakusha Inc.

Published by The Japan Times, Ltd.
5-4, Shibaura 4-chome, Minato-ku, Tokyo 108

Printed in Japan

FOREWORD

At first I planned to call this book *Nihongo-no shukumee*, "The Destiny of the Japanese language." The reasons for that are as follows. When the Japanese think about making Japanese more effective, or about improving language education, they tend to become very theoretical and give little attention to the actual situation. Even disregarding extremists who want to give up on Japanese altogether and adopt English or French, not a few Japanese have a negative attitude toward Japanese because they hold the simplistic view that Japanese is a vague language. Much of their debate confuses characteristics of Japanese usage with characteristics of pronunciation and grammatical structure. There is little meaning in simply making a problem of differences in pronunciation and structure from other languages and elaborating the faults of Japanese; I believe that the important keys for understanding and analysis are to be found, rather, in the way the language is actually used, and in the thinking of the people supporting that usage. Certainly, elements in this thinking underlying spoken Japanese are different in nature from the Western languages, and perhaps Japanese is nonmodern in some respects. However, it is what could be termed the destiny of the Japanese that they are presently using the Japanese language. The Japanese way of using language cannot be changed overnight, but I thought that the first step in Japanese-language reform was to examine how it is actually used in the daily life of the Japanese.

Be that as it may, when I look at the whole book, I see that it largely consists of the presentation of problems, with no proposed course of action. I hope to draw up more concrete proposals as to what should be done at some future time.

Rereading this manuscript, I am struck anew by how much I owe to others. I would like to express my heartfelt gratitude to all those who have helped me and whose names are too numerous to give here — the professors who taught me about language, the Japanese-language students who raised so many problem points, those strangers who kindly gave their opinions at broadcasts and lectures, and so on. In particular, I have no words adequate to express my thanks to Professor Haruhiko Kindaichi, who has displayed an unfailing concern for me over the twenty-five years since I was his student.

I would also like to take this opportunity to express my gratitude to Mr. Shuji Takahashi of Sotakusha, the original publishers of this book, the editorial staff at The Japan Times, and Janet Ashby, the translator of this book, for their unstinting efforts on my behalf.

CONTENTS

Foreword 3
Introduction 7

Chapter 1. Toward an Interest in the Spoken Language 13

The Use of *Konnichi-wa* 13
The Spoken Language and the Written Language 17
'*Jippon*' and '*Juppon*' 20
'Correct' Sentences and Actual Sentences 24
Inner and Outer Values 26

Chapter 2. The Elements of Spoken Japanese ... 29

Motivation and Form of Utterances 29
The Spoken Language and the Flow of Time 33
Sound and Other Important Elements in Language Use 38
Body Movements and Facial Expression When Speaking 42
The Situational Nature of Japanese 45

Chapter 3. The Special Characteristics of Spoken Japanese (1) 53

What Is and Is not Said 53
Who One Does and Does Not Talk to 58
Who One Talks to and Why 63
The Language Behavior of an Average Japanese, Mr. J 68

Chapter 4. The Special Characteristics of Spoken Japanese (2) 81

A Way of Speaking Requiring Two People............... 81
A Form of Expression Which Avoids Opposing Others 86
An Orientation Toward Shared Experience and Knowledge (1) 96
An Orientation Toward Shared Experience and Knowledge (2) 104

Chapter 5. The Special Characteristics of Spoken Japanese (3) 109

The Concern with Relative Advantage and Disadvantage 109
The Concern with Relative Advantage and Disadvantage (2) 116
Interacting with Others in Terms of Higher-Lower Relations... 121
Interacting with Others in Terms of Inner-Outer Relations... 127
The Inner-Outer Philosophy and the Strong Tendency Toward Harmony and Unity................. 133

Chapter 6. Changes in the Life and Language of the Contemporary Japanese....................... 141

Changes in the Content of Communication............... 141
The Means and Environment of Communication 146
The Content and Means of Communication............. 152
Changes in the Speaker.. 162
Expectations Toward Language Education (1) 170
Expectations Toward Language Education (2) 173
References 177
Index.. 178

INTRODUCTION

We human beings are apt to forget the vital importance of those things closest to us, such as air or water. Able to obtain them everyday without any special effort, we take air and water for granted until threatened by pollution or drought.

Language is no exception to this rule of human nature. In Japan, discussion about Chinese characters and English education becomes the occasion for debate over the various shortcomings of the Japanese: the talk turns to how young people today cannot even read novels from the late 19th century which use many Chinese characters, or how students spend ten years learning English in school and still cannot carry on a simple conversation. Certainly these problems are important and should not be neglected.

However, fundamental solutions to problems concerning Chinese characters or English education in Japan will not be found without taking one step back to obtain a broader view of these problems. Bringing water door-to-door in a special truck or installing clean air devices in each household cannot be considered fundamental solutions to drought or air pollution; in the same way we run the risk of not being able to see the real problems in regard to language as well. We must look carefully at the total role language plays in human life.

One important part of this role has long been ignored in Japan — the spoken language. Few Japanese have received formal instruction in spoken Japanese at whatever level of schooling — elementary, junior high, or high school.

In the academic world as well, the feeling is still strong even today that speech does not constitute a proper subject for research. This despite the fact that human life is literally inconceivable without speech and that all research and education is dependent on the spoken as well as the written word.

Why this indifference, and even contempt, should exist toward the spoken language is an interesting topic for speculation. One reason for distrusting the spoken language is its ephemerality: a spoken utterance disappears in an instant. The written language transcends time, making it possible to leave records of one's civilization into eternity. No one can deny the value of writing, but the Japanese have tended to overvalue it, ignoring the interdependence of the written and spoken languages.

Another reason for slighting the spoken language is the role writing has played in supporting the authority of those in the ruling class: those without letters have always been controlled by those with letters. The causes leading to the formation of the social classes may have been political and economic, but the fact remains that the rulers within the established class system could always read and write. Reading and writing have thus served as a passport for advancement in the world, rather than as a key to self-development or individual happiness. The spoken language, however, has had little, if any, connection with authority.

But perhaps the major reason that the spoken language has been relatively forgotten is, paradoxically, its very success as a means of communication. Criticism is often heard about the many mistakes commonly made in the respect language, but spoken Japanese serves perfectly well the communication needs of some 100 million people, a remarkable achievement. The Japanese, however, are as unconscious of this blessing as they are of their abundant water resources.

In the world today there exist places where blood is

being spilled over language, where two or three languages have to be made official languages, and where independence movements spring at least partially from language, as in Quebec or Belgium. Japan is not totally without language problems — the language competency of children returning to Japan after extended stays abroad, the Japanese competency of foreigners living in Japan, the language of the Ainu minority, the regional dialects — but these are minor compared to those in other countries.

A little more interest has been shown in the spoken language recently. There is growing recognition of the need to study the spoken language as a result of criticism attributing a decline in written language skills to changes in life-style and means of communications brought about by the spread of radio, television, and the telephone. The overwhelming influence of language in our daily lives must be acknowledged in regard to education as well. No meaningful results can be expected from schooling carried out in ignorance of the way that language influences the thought processes and concept formation of every individual.

The first step in improving the spoken language skills of the Japanese, and in making their language use as effective as possible in education and social life, is the precise identification of what the spoken language is and how it is used today. To do this, we must abandon all preconceptions of what the spoken language should be, and all prescriptions of the correct or beautiful way of speaking: we must start with an objective observation of what the spoken language is.

Such an examination of the spoken language is, of course, easier said than done, and if carried out properly would fill several volumes. I hope that this one volume will serve as a stepping-stone toward future study of the spoken language, and will be satisfied if it serves to increase interest in spoken Japanese.

Note Concerning Romanization

The romanization used in this book is based on the Hepburn system with the following modifications.

1. When the same vowel occurs consecutively, the letter is repeated rather than using the "-" mark.
    ex. *Tookyoo*   (instead of *Tōkyō*)
2. The sound indicated by the hiragana ん is written with "n" regardless of what sound follows it.
    ex. *shinbun*   (instead of shimbun)
    ex. *shinpai*   (instead of shimpai)

The words connected with hyphens are pronounced as one unit.
    ex. *genki-desu*
    ex. *Soo-desu-ne*

In this book, Japanese names are written in the Japanese order, that is, with the family name first.

JAPANESE: THE SPOKEN LANGUAGE IN JAPANESE LIFE

Chapter 1. Toward an Interest in the Spoken Language

THE USE OF KONNICHI-WA

Konnichi-wa and Ohayoo

  Konnichi-wa (Good day) is a greeting that the Japanese must use thousands of times in the course of a year and hear used tens of thousands of times. But even though they are constantly using konnichi-wa, I doubt if very many Japanese have ever stopped to think about exactly when or how they use it.

  For example, what would the average Japanese reply if asked by a foreigner, "When do you use konnichi-wa?" Most people would probably compare it to similar greetings such as ohayoo (gozaimasu) (Good morning) or konban-wa (Good evening), saying that ohayoo is a greeting used in the morning and konnichi-wa a greeting used in the afternoon. If the foreigner persisted and asked, "And when does morning end and afternoon begin?", the Japanese would probably have difficulty answering. Some would answer that morning goes until around 10 o'clock in the morning, while others would say that it lasts until 11 or even 12 noon.

  Those with some specialized knowledge might reply, "In the mass media or entertainment worlds, ohayoo can be used the first time two people meet that day, even if it's in the evening."

  At this point the majority of Japanese would agree that, some special cases aside, ohayoo is basically a morning greeting and konnichi-wa basically an afternoon greeting.

This information alone, however, is insufficient as a guide to using these two expressions correctly. Although most Japanese are unaware of it, the problem is not one of time at all, but of to whom one is speaking.

'Otoosan konnichi-wa'

The Japanese, in fact, use *ohayoo* and *konnichi-wa* to two distinctly different groups of people, and they will realize this if they think in a little more detail about how they use these two expressions. If they think about particular situations — whether, say, they would use *ohayoo* toward their family when they get up in the morning, toward people in their neighborhood, or toward people at work and, on the other hand, whether they would use *konnichi-wa* in the same situation if it were in the afternoon — then they will realize that there are underlying rules of use that go beyond considerations of time alone.

It is perfectly acceptable to say either *ohayoo* or *ohayoo gozaimasu* to one's parents. But no Japanese would say "*Otoosan, konnichi-wa*" to their father who has come home from work at lunchtime.

This rule of usage is graphically illustrated in a movie made by Ozu Yasujiro some thirty years ago. A husband and wife have found themselves incompatible and obtained a divorce. Their children have lived with the mother. When they meet their father after some years, the greeting that comes out is *konnichi-wa*. This *konnichi-wa* makes perfectly clear the relationship between this father and his children, for in a family with a normal home life children would never use *konnichi-wa* toward their father. The use of *konnichi-wa* only becomes possible when they are not living under one roof, that is, when he has become an outsider.

It does seem that one can use *konnichi-wa* to the people in one's neighborhood, although probably not to everyone without exception. But what about one's co-workers at the office, the people with whom one works everyday from morning to night? Suppose for some reason or other a Japanese comes to work at a little after noon. When he steps through the door, will he greet his co-workers with *konnichi-wa*? Of course this is not inconceivable, but in most cases a Japanese will try to use some other expression instead such as, *"Yaa, okurete-shimatte"* (Sorry to be late) or *"Kyoo-wa, kyuu ni yoo ga dekite-shimatta mono-de"* (I got held up by something that came up suddenly today). If he were to use *konnichi-wa*, this would indicate a particular attitude toward the others; the most typical instances of someone using *konnichi-wa* at a work place are a deliveryman bringing some take-out food there or some other tradesman.

This relationship between *ohayoo* and *konnichi-wa* also exists between *oyasumi-nasai* (Good night) and *konban-wa* (Good evening); that is, *oyasumi-nasai* is used to persons both inside and outside one's in-group and *konban-wa* to persons outside it. Few Japanese, however, are aware of the distinct differences in usage of these two pairs of expressions.

This sort of distinction is by no means limited to Japanese. Although the Japanese tend to think that the English greetings "Good morning," "Good afternoon," "Good evening," and "Good night" are used according to time alone, there are undoubtedly differences in use depending on the situation as well. The Chinese expression *ni hao* has also become popular in Japan recently, and even small children know this as the equivalent of *konnichi-wa*. But this *ni hao* also has certain qualifications on its use: like *konnichi-wa* it is used, in contrast to *ohayoo*, to persons outside one's in-group but is even more formal; the Chinese do not use *ni hao* toward those who are very close, such as family members. If the Japanese learn *ni hao* and use it in all situations toward the Chinese they meet, the very real possibility exists that they will always be frozen at one level of relations with the Chinese; they may all unknowingly be faced with a barrier of their own making.

'Nihongo-ga ojoozu-desu-ne'

This danger is also present for foreigners studying Japanese. For example, American students learn *konnichi-wa*. Thinking that here is a way to greet people in a friendly fashion, they start using it indiscriminately toward the Japanese students at their school, the Japanese they work with, and the family they live with. But contrary to their intentions, this use of *konnichi-wa* is one part of a problem many foreigners experience in Japan.

The Japanese seem to be very indulgent toward foreigners, especially at first, and many beginning students of Japanese become irritated when the Japanese they meet unfailingly tell them, *"Zuibun ojoozu-desu ne"* (You speak Japanese very well) when they say anything at all in Japanese, no matter how faltering. They suspect that this false praise of their broken Japanese actually expresses a hidden contempt of foreigners, the feeling that a foreigner speaking Japanese is a curiosity on a par with a speaking dog. Foreigners also feel that they run into another wall when they become very good in Japanese and can talk quite naturally; they say that to be accepted by the Japanese, it is better to speak in poor Japanese. This, however, is a mistaken conclusion.

It is perfectly true that a barrier exists which frustrates their efforts to break through to closer relations with the Japanese they meet. The use of *konnichi-wa* referred to above is one key to this problem. As long as foreigners use *konnichi-wa* with the Japanese family they are living with, they will always remain an outsider. The Japanese themselves will stop using *konnichi-wa* as they gradually become closer, aside from special situations such as the presence of a third party. And the dropping of this expression between two persons serves to mutually confirm the shortened distance between them.

Taking language for granted

All Japanese can freely use *konnichi-wa* and *ohayoo*, *konban-wa* and *oyasumi-nasai*, and they think they know the meaning of these expressions. But as we have seen, if they should stop to think about just when they use them, or to whom they use them, they may well be shocked to realize how unconsciously they rely on language in their daily lives. This is, of course, not limited to the Japanese alone; all peoples pay little conscious attention to their native tongue. I often hear about Japanese exchange students in the United States teaching English grammar to Americans, or receiving better grades in grammar classes than the American students. The Japanese, however, as we will explore in this book, seem to be especially lacking in the habit of reflecting on language, the spoken language in particular.

THE SPOKEN LANGUAGE AND THE WRITTEN LANGUAGE

Mistress: "Sawadi", servant: "....?"

Sakamoto Yasuaki, an assistant professor at the Institute for the Study of Languages and Cultures of Asia and Africa, tells a story about the Japanese in Thailand that supports my charge that the Japanese are not in the habit of reflecting objectively on spoken language. Sakamoto, in fact, wonders if it might not be better for

Japanese *not* to study Thai before going there to live. He explains that the wives of Japanese trading company employees in Thailand learn before leaving Japan that the Thai greeting corresponding to *konnichi-wa* or *ohayoo* is *sawadi*. Accordingly, on getting up in the morning, a wife will say *sawadi* to her Thai servants, but get no greeting in return. She feels they are being rude to her since the servants do exchange greetings among themselves. But in actuality *sawadi* is not the exact equivalent of either *ohayoo* or *konnichi-wa*: *sawadi* is not used by someone of higher rank to someone of lower rank unless the person of lower rank has first greeted that person with *sawadi*, and the person of higher rank is returning this greeting.

Consequently, when, as in the case of the Japanese wives, the higher-ranking person first says *sawadi*, it is a reprimand to the lower-ranking person for not greeting the higher-ranking person quickly enough. Since the Japanese wives did not fully understand the use of *sawadi*, they unwittingly confused their Thai servants and themselves received a mistaken impression of the Thais. Professor Sakamoto has given us one more example of a little knowledge being a dangerous thing.

The Japanese complex toward writing

Discussion about the spoken language in Japan — usually about respect language — is very limited; the written language occupies the center of the stage, and great attention is paid to problems concerning *kanji* (the Chinese characters), *kana* (the phonetic syllabary), and *romaji* (the roman letters used to transcribe Japanese). Much heated debate takes place over *kanji* in particular: for example, what *kanji* are correct and which *kanji* should be selected as official *kanji* for daily use (the *toyo kanji*). The schools earnestly teach *kanji* to their students, and parents tend to think that memorization of *kanji* is equivalent to learning Japanese language skills. The problems of *kanji* — of reading, writing, and even the order of writing *kanji* — are dealt with in microscopic detail: for example, should the left vertical, downward line constituting the second stroke in the character for village (*mura*; 村) have a slight flourish to the left at the bottom or end with no flourish?

And debate over the proper order of strokes in writing characters is not restricted to *kanji* alone. In the fall of 1978, debate raged in the newspapers for two or three weeks about the order of strokes in writing roman letters given in junior high school English textbooks published in Japan. Writers protested that no clear instruction was given about the order — or, more precisely, there was instruction, but it differed according to the text. When Americans and Englishmen were asked for their opinion, most of them said it made no difference in what order a letter was written. I think the very fact that a debate could take place over where one should start when writing an E, an A, or whatever illustrates very well the Japanese complex about written characters and their attitude toward language.

The Japanese indifference toward the spoken language

Though the Japanese worry so much about the written word, they show almost total indifference toward the spoken word. How many teachers in elementary or junior high school criticize their students' pronunciation and make them pronounce something over and over or give them special homework? A speech class is necessary for receiving a teaching certificate, but little practical training or guidance is given teachers in regard to the spoken word.

We can see this attitude once again in the Japanese handling of foreign names. Most Japanese, myself included, find it difficult to remember foreign names and, when introduced to foreigners, will ask them to repeat their names or to spell their names, thus putting them into the written language. And often the Japanese will not even make this much effort but simply resign themselves to not catching the name. Foreigners in the early stages of learning Japanese also have trouble with Japanese names due to differences in the sound system of Japanese or to a lack of familiarity with Japanese names. When I say my name, Mizutani, foreigners will often ask "Mirutani?" or "Metani?" But, unlike the Japanese, they seem to be able to get it right on first hearing once they have become more used to Japanese names and more proficient in Japanese. The Japanese, however, still seem to be weak in hearing and remembering foreign names even after they have long studied English and can converse in it comfortably.

Evident here is one part of the Japanese psychology — always being ill at ease unless they can see something in writing. The reliance on the exchange of name cards in Japan is one more illustration of this attitude.

'JIPPON' AND 'JUPPON'

Juu + hon = jippon

I know of an elementary school student who was marked wrong for writing 分 instead of 分 for the Chinese character for minute in "ten minutes"; as noted above, the Japanese are extremely sensitive in any matter concerning the written language. But in contrast, it seems that they are very loose as far as pronunciation is concerned. For example, should *juu* (十 ; ten) plus *hon* (本 ; the counter used for long, cylindrical objects such as pencils, bottles, or cigarettes) be pronounced *jippon* or *juppon*? Which one is used in textbooks and the like? And finally, is there a difference between its written form and how it is commonly pronounced —and do the Japanese even consider whether this difference might exist?

As a matter of fact, although it hardly ever appears in printed materials, I found through investigation that *juppon* (十本) is overwhelmingly preponderant in everyday speech. There were some differences according to region and age group, and the rate of young people saying *juppon* was especially high. Recent dictionaries, however, though listing both pronunciations, give *jippon* as the standard pronunciation.

Persons pronouncing this *juppon* undoubtedly do so since it comes from *juu*, but on purely historical grounds *jippon* is correct. The following explanation is from Shiraishi Daiji's *Hyojungo Jiten* (Dictionary of Standard Japanese).[1] Certain words originally written *shifu* or *rifu* have become *shuu* or *ryuu* — as in 執 in 執念 (*shuunen*; deep attachment, tenacity) or 立 in 建立 (*konryuu*; building, erection) — but when followed by certain consonants, they become *shi* or *ri* with a doubling of that consonant — as in 北条執権 (*Hoojoo shikken*; a Hojo family regent) or 立派な人 (*rippana hito*; a fine person). *Juu* belongs to this group; that is, although it is now pronounced *juu*, it was originally *jifu*. Therefore before *hon*, it becomes *jippon* rather than *juppon*.

But which of the above should be regarded as the more serious problem — the correct way to write the character 分 (*fun*; minute) or the fact that no one seems aware of the difference between how *jippon* is written and how it is actually pronounced?

The Japanese separation of writing and speech

An interesting example of the Japanese attitude toward writing and speaking appeared in a recent book of research on Chinese vocabulary, *Chuugokugo to taioosuru kango* (Chinese and the equivalent Sino-Japanese words) from the Waseda University Institute of Language Teaching.[2] Aimed at making the study of Japanese by Chinese-speakers as efficient as possible, this book tries to clarify the exact relationship existing between Japanese and Chinese; specifically, it discusses such problems as Chinese characters used in Chinese but not in Japanese and characters used in both languages but with different meanings. One of the persons involved in this project, Takebe Yoshiaki, noticed a curious phenomenon.

He writes that when Japanese saw a Chinese character used in Chinese, they inferred its meaning from its use in Japanese, thereby opening the way for possible misunderstanding. However, the Chinese proceeded differently: when reading Japanese, they voiced the characters within their heads and if they were not used in Chinese, they excluded them as different words.

This example brings into clear contrast the different expectations the Japanese have toward the Chinese characters used by both peoples or, in slightly different terms, the different role the characters play within the two languages. In Chinese, a Chinese character has only one pronunciation or tone. In this sense, writing and speech are in a one-to-one correspondence in Chinese. But in Japanese, each Chinese character has several readings: it has *on* (Sino-Japanese) readings and *kun* (native Japanese) readings — and in certain cases there may be over a hundred different possible readings! The correspondence of character and reading is not one-to-one, leading to the separation of character and speech in Japanese. It is a given of linguistics that language is fundamentally speech, but it is questionable to what extent the Japanese can overcome their indifference toward speech and comprehend this principle.

似合う is not niau

For example, I had the following experience some twenty years ago when I was teaching Japanese to Americans. One day when I was correcting their pronunciation of the model sentence *"Kimono-ga yoku niau hito-da"* (It is a person who looks well in kimono), a student said, "The 'a' in *niau* isn't really 'a', is it?" but I could not understand what in the world that student meant. No matter how hard I thought about it, the "a" of *niau* still seemed to me to be "a" and not some other sound. But I was wrong. When said naturally, "a" following "i" is actually pronounced "ya" so that, just as this student had pointed out, *niau* is pronounced *niyau* and *miai* (the first meeting for a possible marriage) is pronounced *miyai*. The Japanese, however, hear these as *niau* and *miai* and are completely unaware that they are any different from the pure "a" used in other cases.

Since it is very difficult for the Japanese to perceive this "ya" in common words like *niau* or *miai*, they should try pronouncing some madeup, nonsense word like "utogaria" instead. No matter how hard they try to say "a," a person standing next to them will hear this as "ya." And it is only then that they are fully convinced of this sound change.

I will give only a few more instances of the widespread ignorance of the actual pronunciation of Japanese in Japan. Many people do not realize that, although written with different characters, "ぢ" and "じ" are both pronounced "ji" [dʒi], or that "づ" and "ず" are both pronounced "zu" [dzu]. Similarly, very few notice that the pronunciation of the "u" sound in "tsu" is actually quite different from the other "u" sounds, such as "ku" or "pu." Most adults think a child's pronunciation of *itsutsu* (five) as "ichuchu" is far from the correct sound, but the adult "tsu" is actually the aberrant sound. Finally, the Japanese often say that they cannot say the English "r" and "l," but few are aware that a large percentage of the Japanese pronounce the consonant of *ra* or *ro* very close to the English "l."

'CORRECT' SENTENCES AND ACTUAL SENTENCES

It's a correct sentence, but . . . .

The gap between preconceptions and the reality of the spoken language does not exist for pronunciation alone, but for every aspect of the spoken language. For example, consider the sentence, *"Ocha-o doozo nonde-kudasai"* (literally, Please drink the tea). Is this a good Japanese sentence? It is certainly a grammatically correct sentence, but would the Japanese actually use it in their daily lives? If not, what do they say to express this thought?

If used to tell someone to drink some tea, this sentence has a coercive tone — drink that tea or else! But it somehow does not seem appropriate even in a command situation, for example a doctor telling a patient to drink tea to cure some digestive ailment. Much less would one say *"nonde kudasai"* (please drink it) when offering tea to a guest.

One would say *"Ocha-o doozo"* (literally, the tea please) or simply *"doozo"* (please) instead. In an extreme case, one might not even say *"doozo,"* but simply hand over the filled teacup to the guest in silence.

This sentence, however — *"Ocha-o doozo nonde-kudasai"* — will usually be accepted without comment in a classroom in Japan as a direct translation from English. Although the original sentence was spoken English, there appears to be little thought given to whether the translation is spoken Japanese or not.

What is the answer to "How much is it"?

The sentences used in spoken Japanese are clearly different from those used in written Japanese; this difference is not simply a matter of the form of the sentence but also the kind of response elicited by a given sentence. The Japanese, however, seem to be as unconscious of the exact process of the formation of sentences within the give-and-take of actual conversation as they are of the different forms of spoken and written sentences. For example, take the question, *"Kore-wa ikura desu-ka"* (How much is this?). When used in the most common situation, a customer asking a clerk in a store, the expected response is a price, such as "It's ¥3000" or "That's ¥5000."

But is this actually the case? When a research team investigating conversation from Tsukuba University headed by Ouchi Shigeo went out and asked this question, they received very few direct responses of this sort. Instead, the clerks or shopkeepers said "Which one?" (*Dore*), "What?" (*Nan desu-ka*), or made some completely different response. Some of these answers demonstrate a particularly Japanese attitude: in response to "How much is this?" came "Oh, that's very cheap," (*A, taihen oyasuku natte-imasu-yo*) or "Oh, that's on special today" (*A, sore-wa toku-ni saabisu-no shina-de-gozaimasu*). That is, rather than responding directly to the needs of the questioner, they expressed their own concerns as shopkeepers in their assertion of the worth of the goods. These are very typical responses, and, indeed, Americans who have been studying Japanese often say that clerks in Japan never answer their questions but only push the merchandise on them, saying this product is good or that piece of clothing is very becoming to you.

When thinking about language problems, we tend to forget that language is not simply the words that we say or write down on paper, but is a human-made, socially based system. If we do not move beyond the surface level of what is expressed in speech or writing, or beyond the slightly more abstract conception of what conversation should be, then we will remain unable to precisely grasp and analyze the reality of what the spoken language actually is.

INNER AND OUTER VALUES

Recognizing only the values of others

Written or printed words are, of course, more easily verifiable than spoken words as one can read them over and over. In contrast, spoken words leave no record, making it difficult to catch hold of the spoken language. No one can deny the value of the written word and of the writing system itself.

However, its ephemerality alone does not account for the low value set on the spoken language in Japan: the Japanese have a general tendency to value what is far away more highly than what is close at hand. I recognize the value of studying foreign cultures, poring over the classics, and searching for models and guidance for our own lives in the great works of literature. We must not forget, however, the necessity of being true to ourselves. It is impossible to achieve any true learning or realize any truly productive work as long as we slight our own ability and judgment. The custom of learning from others is so strong in Japan that some people even feel it presumptuous to value what they themselves feel or think — and we can see this attitude on the national level as well. But valuing only written masterworks and directing all one's energies into reading, studying, and imitating these works leads to the loss of one's own individuality; such study is painful and ultimately sterile. And is it too farfetched to think that herein lies one cause of the Japanese neglect of the spoken language?

When I think back on my own schooling, I realize that my language training almost exclusively consisted of being given certain selected passages, and of my passively studying, absorbing, and memorizing these. From time to time the problem of making this knowledge and information relevant to the individual so that it could become true food for growth was raised, but this was never dealt with as a practical problem. Sometimes the cry would be heard from the intellectuals to take the spoken language seriously, but it always remained the cry of a few and aroused no widespread concern or support. I think it is time Japan developed a sense of values giving equal importance to the individual and to the society as a whole. Until this new orientation takes place, it is impossible to expect Japan to become a truly creative and productive society.

The true importance of studying foreign languages

I have been writing about the relationship of the individual and society, but the same thing can be said about the relationship of Japan and the world as well. One cause for the national lack of confidence is the study of the cultures, technology, and languages of chosen advanced nations, the English-speaking ones in particular, solely in order to catch up with or to overcome them. The time has now come to think seriously about drastically reforming English and other foreign-language education — as well as Japanese-language education — in Japan.

I am not saying that the spoken language is more important than the written language, but that the Japanese should stop ignoring the interrelationship between the spoken and the written languages, for, as one cultivates and hones the spoken language, the written language becomes more exact and polished, and as one studies the written language, the spoken language becomes a richer means of communication. If the Japanese, however, continue to concentrate on the written language in total disregard of the spoken language, and on the form of the written characters in total disregard of their pronunciation, then all the labor they exert in improving their language skills will not contribute one whit to their spoken sentences; that is the crux of the problem.

Chapter 2. The Elements of Spoken Japanese

MOTIVATION AND FORM OF UTTERANCES

'A, ame-da' and 'A, ame-da-yo'

As discussed in Chapter 1, the sentences actually said in everyday life differ in form from written ones, and a large disparity exists between how the Japanese think they talk and how they actually talk. The spoken language clearly differs considerably from the written language and also from what we might call the "voiced written language," i.e., the language used in radio and television newscasts.

We can imagine many different types of conversations, but no matter what the situation might be there is always some particular motivation for our utterances. At times we express our personal thoughts or emotions in a monologue. At other times we want to convey some information to a friend or stimulate someone to take a particular action. But although a motive is always present for each utterance, the form of the utterance does not always coincide perfectly with that motive.

For example, suppose a Japanese sitting inside happened to look outside and see that it had started to rain. He might put this into words and say "A, ame-da" (Oh, it's raining), an utterance that could take place even if he were alone. If he was informing someone else in the family that it had started to rain, we would expect the form to change to the more emphatic "A, ame-da-yo" (It's raining!). Or, if there were clothes hanging outside to dry, he might say, *"Ame-da-yo. Sentakumono-o torikonde-yo"* (It's raining! Bring in the clothes). These three different forms — muttering to himself with no thought of conveying his thoughts or feelings to another person, informing another person, and telling another person to bring about a desired action — are illustrated in Figure 1. If, however, we look at what Japanese actually say in such a situation, this one-to-one correspondence of motive and form of speech act is clearly not always preserved.

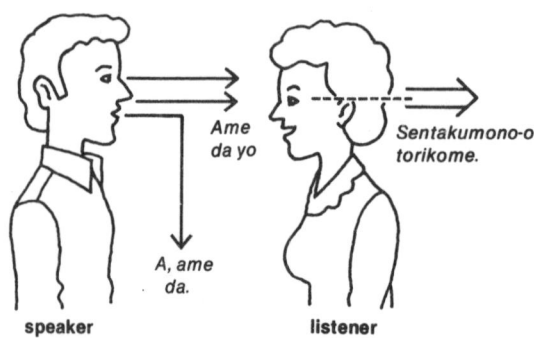

Figure 1

For example, when one wants the listener to bring in the clothes, it is not necessary to say so specifically. One might simply say, *"Ame-ga futte-kita-yo"* (It's started raining!), and the listener will think, "Oh, that means he/she wants me to bring in the clothes." Of course, the following exchange is also possible.

"Ame-da-yo." (It's raining!)
"Dakara nan-na-no." (So what?)
"Sentakumono-ga hoshite-aru-ja nai-ka, wakaran-no-ka." (What's the matter with you? You have clothes hanging out to dry, don't you?)

But even in this case, it is clear that *"Ame-da-yo"* actually implied, "Bring in the clothes." It was the failure to understand this implicit meaning that called forth the implied *"Wakaran-no-ka, ame-de sentaku-mono-ga nureru-dewa nai-ka"* (Don't you understand? The clothes will get wet in the rain, won't they?).

The motivation of 'Samui-nee'

This discrepancy between motive and form of utterance is found in many different situations. For example, a higher-up comes into a room where several people are working and mutters, *"Samui-nee"* (It's cold in here). This may simply express the thought *"Soto-wa samui-n-da-yo"* (Boy, it's really cold out today), or, on the other hand, it may be intended to bring about a certain action on the part of the people in the room. In the latter case, the higher-up entered the room and found it cold. Then he noticed that the window was open and wondered why. The reader might think that he could just say, *"Samui-ja nai-ka, sono mado-o shimete-kure"* (Aren't you cold? Please close that window). Speech acts, however, do not take place in a vacuum, and he must consider the human relationships involved. He therefore avoids giving a direct order and says *"Samui-nee"* instead, hoping that one of those present will understand his unspoken meaning, notice the window is open, and close it, perhaps saying something like *"A, soo-ka, mado-ga akete-atta"* (Oh that's right. The window's open).

Of course, not all Japanese use this indirect form of expression to try to bring about some desired action; some will express their wishes directly in the form of an order or request. The choice of a direct or indirect form of expression can be thought of as a problem of individual difference, but the preference for one or the other is a general tendency within a given language.

The gap between the motive and the actual form of the utterance is not unique to the Japanese language, but my feeling is that this gap is wider in the case of Japanese than, say, English. At any rate, it is safe to say that in the majority of cases, a Japanese will hesitate to explicitly ask someone to do something unless some special relationship exists between the two persons to make that likely.

Consideration toward others

Consideration toward others, *omoiyari*, is a major element in this Japanese dislike of conveying a message through words alone, as will be discussed in more detail in Chapter 3. Here we can note that this consideration is an effort to avoid hurting others or, from a different angle, the avoidance of plainly putting into words the psychological state of *amae*, a presuming upon the kindness of others. A speaker imposing some task upon another, therefore, will seek to have that action done at the will of the other. In extreme terms, the speaker can savor a joy that the listener has understood without the necessity of putting everything into words.

The way of using words to express oneself may play a different role in communication, or verbal expressions may have a different functional load, in different languages. This difference can also exist within the same language, and the users of Japanese can show individual differences in language use as well as differences according to the group or substratum of society to which they belong. At the very least, the presumption that the form of an utterance is identical to its motive is obviously untenable.

THE SPOKEN LANGUAGE AND THE FLOW OF TIME

Does one have to use complete sentences in Japanese?

Japanese is often accused of being vague because the meaning of a sentence is not clear until the end. It is true that there are sentences in which one cannot be sure of what the speaker is trying to say until one listens to the very end, as in *"Hitori-de iku koto-wa nai-kamo shirenai nado-to-wa iwanai wake-dewa nai"* (It is not the case that I would not say something like I might not go alone).

However, that is not valid as a general statement about the Japanese language. Although this kind of sentence does exist in Japanese, one only rarely encounters it in everyday conversation. In fact, this type of expression is usually used only when one is in a particularly perverse mood and deliberately sets out to annoy the listener.

In spoken Japanese, the sentence ending is relatively unimportant. And to the extent that the ending is unimportant, the beginning of the sentence becomes more important: this principle is the subject of this section.

This principle was illustrated in a personal experiment I tried one day with foreign students of Japanese and Japanese students. I prepared pairs of sentences in which the neutral beginning of a sentence was followed by either an expression of approval or an expression of opposition or hesitation, as in

> *"Soo-desu-ne. Zehi soo shimashoo."* (Well. Let us do so by all means.) and
> *"Soo-desu-ne, kondo-ni shimasen-ka."* (Well, why don't we decide later?).

Then I had the students listen to these sentences one

portion at a time, asking them about the meaning of the sentence and the motive of the speaker. The majority of the Japanese students were able to predict fairly well the second part of the first sentence (*Zehi soo shimashoo*) before hearing it; indeed some were able to do so after only hearing as far as "*Soo de* . . ." But although the foreign students were quite advanced in Japanese and had read recent Japanese books as part of their studies, almost none of them could even guess at the meaning of the second sentence in the set after hearing the first one all the way through to the end.

In addition to raising questions about the methods used to teach the spoken language to foreign students, this experiment revealed that, surprisingly enough, all of the Japanese students could predict the rest of the sentence after hearing the beginning; that is, they could guess the intention of the utterance, whether the rest was in the affirmative or the negative.

How could the Japanese students guess at the ending of the sentence so quickly? That is possible because the information of approval or rejection is encoded in the sounds of the utterances of the spoken language. As far as the spoken language is concerned, therefore, we can reject the idea that the meaning of the sentence is not determined until the end.

The spoken language is made up of a series of voiced sounds produced under the restrictions of time. For effective communication to take place, it is only natural that the most important information will be conveyed in the early part of the sentence.

The spoken language obviously differs from the written language which has, by definition, been frozen on the page, and if we look at the clues of the voiced sounds from a temporal perspective, we can discover many new aspects of expression in the Japanese language.

Written sentences, spoken sentences

Consider the sentence,

"*Densha-ga okureta-ni shite-mo, moo kuru koro-da*"
(Even if the train is late, it's time [he/she/it/they] were coming),

one given as an example of a spoken sentence in an intermediate level textbook for foreign students of Japanese. When asked what the subject of *kuru* (come) is, the majority of foreign students will reply *"densha"* (the train), and they find it hard to believe that they are wrong.

When Japanese are asked the same question, the majority think a little while and then reply, "It's not the train." But occasionally one will say, "It's the train that's coming." Most of the latter are young people, but this does not seem to reflect a consistently different feeling for language according to age.

When the method of presentation is changed, and the sentence is heard rather than seen, all agree that it is not the train that is coming but rather the person or persons who are expected to come.

Sound is the foundation of the spoken language, the building blocks for communication through words. Although no one would think of denying this obvious truth, it is all too easily overlooked in discussions about the spoken language. And when one sees a written sentence, whether it is in *kanji* and *kana* or all in *katakana*, it is difficult to form an image of how it would sound spoken. Even if one does not pick out the characters one by one, it is easy to fall into the habit of dividing it into phrases rather than grasping it as one unit.

In each sentence, there is a pattern of placing high sounds among the phrases that I call prominence. In the sentence above, if the prominence used leaves no pause between *densha-ga* and *okureta-ni shite-mo*, and has *densha-ga* pronounced higher, then it is clear that the subject of *kuru* is not the train. If the sentence were to be divided in two and the *ga* of *densha-ga* replaced with *wa*, this relationship between the two parts becomes obvious. This example sentence can thus be discussed in terms of the difference of *wa* and *ga* as well as of the role of prominence with which we are more concerned here.

The major reason that the foreign students were not able to understand this sentence — *"Densha-ga okureta-ni shite-mo, moo kuru koro-da"* — is that they could not imagine the situation in which it is used. They did not understand that two people — or possibly one person talking to himself — are talking about how some third party has not arrived at the arranged time. In other words, in order to understand this sentence, one has to imagine the content of the conversation before this sentence, to grasp the context of the sentence.

If the sentence had been, *"Densha-ga okureta-ni shite-mo, moo kare-ga kuru koro-da"* (Even if the train is late, it's time he came), those intermediate students of Japanese would have understood it without any trouble. However, if they carefully study natural, high-frequency expressions like the former sentence, foreign students will be able to understand sentences in which understood words are omitted, one important characteristic of spoken Japanese.

Understanding sentences in the continuum of time

The form of the sentence discussed above—*Densha-ga okureta-ni shite-mo, moo kuru koro-da* — will be modified according to what comes before it. If two people are waiting together for someone else and one of them says *"Densha-ga jiko-de nijippun-gurai okuretatte, rajio-de itteta-yo"* (They said on the radio that there was an accident and the trains are running about twenty minutes late), then it is possible to reply *"Okureta-ni shite-*

mo, moo kuru koro-da" (Even if [it] is late, it's time [he/she/they] came).

If this latter sentence is removed from its context and thought about as an isolated sentence, the subject of "come" is ambiguous — it could be a friend or the train or something else. In this context, however, it is clear that it is the train that is late and a friend that is coming.

Sentences like these which lack an explicitly stated subject are the bête noire of foreign students learning Japanese. Some of these foreigners say defensively that the Japanese language is illogical and so on — and some Japanese agree with them. One should not, however, distort how Japanese is actually used when teaching it to foreigners. Many of them will want to put in many more subjects than necessary because of a dislike of ambiguity, but this should not be permitted; often a Japanese expression is complete without explicitly stating the subject, and in this case, the sentence will take on a special meaning if the subject is expressed.

"Uchi-ni kaettara sugu denwa-suru-yo" ([I]'ll call [you] as soon as [I] get home) is a perfectly ordinary sentence. But if one should put in the pronouns and say *"Boku-ga uchi-ni kaettara, sugu-ni kimi-ni denwa-suru-yo"*, it implies that one is specifically choosing "I" out of the number of possible people returning and, similarly, that there are people other than "you" to whom one could be telephoning.

Consider the following conversation.

A: *Techoo-o uchi-e wasurete-kite-shimatta-n-de, itsu-da-ka hakkiri shinai-n-da.* ([I] left my memorandum book at home so [I]'m not sure when it is.)
B: *Komatta-naa, kyoojuu-ni shiritai-n-da-ga.* ([I]'m sorry but [I] really need to know today.)

A: *Sore-jaa, uchi-e kaettara sugu denwa-suru-yo.* (In that case, [I]'ll call you as soon as [I] get home.)

If one unnecessarily inserted *boku* (I) in this last sentence and said *"Boku-ga uchi-e kaettara"*, it would impress the listener with the strong self-assertiveness of the speaker.

There are, of course, cases where it is necessary to clearly express *boku* and say *Boku-ga uchi-e kaettara*. However, it is one of the special characteristics of spoken Japanese that information already conveyed to the listener in the course of the conversation is not explicitly expressed unless there is some special reason for doing so. It is thus important in teaching Japanese as a foreign language to give special attention to teaching students to understand spoken sentences in the continuum of time rather than as separate, discrete units.

SOUND AND OTHER IMPORTANT ELEMENTS IN LANGUAGE USE

I am the teacher＝This is a nose

I have already stated above that the spoken language is made up of sounds and, further, that it must be grasped in the context of unfolding time.

When we are actually using the spoken language, however, except for the special case of the telephone, we also make extensive use of extralinguistic elements in communication, such as facial expression, body movement, and everyday objects like teacups or cigarettes, as well as of the conditions present in the physical setting of a particular speech act. According to the relationship between the people involved or the situation, just raising the hand can mean "Good morning" or "OK, I understand." Since this kind of sign or signal is not in the strict sense linguistic, they are usually thought of divorced from language. In addition to the signs and signals independent of language are the body movements and facial expressions which accompany an utterance. These have been the object of some research, but little attention has been given to the sheer size of the role they play in spoken language. This oversight has led to some weak points in the teaching of Japanese as a foreign language.

The direct method, in which the instructor uses Japanese as much as possible and avoids using the native language of the students, be it English or Chinese, is widely used in the teaching of Japanese to foreigners. One problem with this method is illustrated in the following anecdote.

In one of their very first lessons, an instructor was teaching his pupils the sentences

Watakushi-wa gakusei-desu. (I am a student.)
Watakushi-wa sensei-desu. (I am a teacher.)
Anata-wa gakusei-desu. (You are a student.)

Accordingly, he entered the classroom, pointed at himself — i.e., he pointed to his nose with his index finger as the Japanese do when saying, "Who, me?" — and repeated *"Watakushi-wa sensei-desu"*, *"Watakushi-wa sensei-desu."* Then he pointed to the students and said *"Anata-wa gakusei-desu."* But it turned out that from his gesture the students thought that *Watakushi-wa sensei-desu* meant "This is a nose"!

Not many peoples in the world indicate themselves by pointing to their noses as the Japanese do. And it is obvious that people who point toward their chest with their hand to indicate themselves, as English-speakers do, will find some other meaning in pointing to one's nose with one's index finger.

By the same token, the Japanese will also have their own reaction to the body movements of foreigners; in particular, they will find their pointing to be strange and, at times, even offensive. For example, pointing at someone while talking to him or her makes a poor impression on the Japanese. Although individual differences exist, Americans and other foreigners will sometimes point at the person they are talking to when they are trying to convince him or her of something or when they are especially intent on conveying some information. This gesture looks very strong and aggressive to the Japanese, but for Americans it is not all that strong and does not imply any forcing of one's emotions onto the other person.

The Japanese bow while shaking hands

More than twenty years ago when I first began teaching Japanese to foreigners, I had the following experience. When I had finished my first hour of teaching and was preparing to leave the classroom, an American coed called out to me. She was taller than me and looked quite imposing to me as she started walking toward me. As I watched, she came closer and closer until it seemed that I would touch her if I raised my hand. It was my first class and I had no confidence about how it had gone so that even though she did not look angry, I wondered if she might not be going to complain about something. Her facial expression was not all that forbidding, but she came so close to me that I involuntarily took a step backward. But when I did that she took another step closer to me. Since the distance between us was too short, I felt like I was being pursued by that tall student towering over me, and I retreated a second time. However, the blackboard was behind me so that I could not withdraw any further. I felt uneasy and made an effort to smile, but the expression on my face must have been rather strained. But she obliviously moved closer once again and said that she had a question. This question turned out to be about some grammatical point or other and was not the complaint or special request that I had been half-expecting.

This experience was an unsettling one for me because the distance between us was much shorter than that normal between a Japanese man and woman; this was the first time I had ever talked with a foreign woman under these circumstances. After that I observed American women talking comfortably with men and I noticed that, generally speaking, the distance between them was much shorter than that left between Japanese under the same circumstances. Individual preferences and the like make it impossible to say that exactly X centimeters are left between the sexes in the two countries, but it is safe to say that this distance is shorter in the United States than in Japan.

In fact, this acceptable distance is also connected with the way that the Japanese shake hands. It is said that the Japanese often bow while shaking hands, a habit many find undesirable. The supposition that they do this because the custom of bowing came first probably has some truth to it. If we approach this problem from another angle, however, it is also possible that this bowing occurs because the Japanese stand at a distance from each other that is not quite right for handshaking. Properly speaking, when shaking hands, the two people come quite close to each other and then raise and extend their right hand; they are close enough to be able to easily place their left hand on the other's shoulder or embrace each other. The Japanese, however, shrink from standing that close to each other. They unconsciously stop one step short and stretch out their arm. At that distance, it would be impossible to place their hand on the other's shoulder; it is, rather, a proper distance for bowing. When standing at this distance, the elbow of the outstretched arm is almost straight and, more than a handshake, this stance leads to lowering one's head with one's arm extended. And as one stretches out one's arm, the hips are lowered slightly backward, naturally leading into a bow.

BODY MOVEMENTS AND FACIAL EXPRESSION WHEN SPEAKING

Facial expression as a greeting

I wrote earlier that voiced sounds are harder for us to grasp than the written word. But it is just as, or even more difficult, for us to be aware of the facial expression or body movements accompanying speech. And to the extent that we are unaware of such behavior, we are apt to underestimate its importance in supporting the spoken sounds.

In the fall of 1974, I spent two weeks helping teach Japanese to American students at Cornell University. One hour I was putting the finishing touches to a greeting that they had studied: *Hajimemashite*. _____ *de gozaimasu. Doozo yoroshiku.* (How do you do? My name is _____. I'm pleased to meet you). The students had already practiced it many times with their text and language tapes and were now prepared to actually use it for the first time with a Japanese who had just arrived from Japan. Accordingly, I had them suppose they were meeting me for the first time and greet me appropriately one by one. The first student greeted me: *"Watakushi-wa Jonson-de gozaimasu. Hajimete ome-ni kakarimasu. Doozo yoroshiku onegai-itashimasu."* (My name is Johnson. How do you do? I'm pleased to meet you.)

This first effort was really a smooth, clearly pronounced greeting. I was a little surprised, however, because although the form of the greeting was beautifully mastered, that student's facial expression was not the proper one for a greeting.

One often hears that the Japanese have little facial expression, and it is true that if one watches Americans talking together, all the parts of their face — the eyebrows, cheeks, eyes, etc. — are moving quite vigorously. Compared to that, I had thought the Japanese might well be called expressionless, but I learned then that this judgment was not completely accurate.

Those American students were so expressionless that I instructed them: Smile while you say it. And watch my face and say in accordance with my reaction, *"Hajimemashite. Doozo yoroshiku. _____ de gozaimasu."* But it turned out to be very difficult to make them smile at the beginning of the greeting. I tried going out of the room and coming back in, instructing them to check my face and then smile, but that had no greater success. I just could not make those students understand that smiling is part of the greeting for the Japanese. Of course Americans also smile and laugh; they laugh loudly when happy and look worried when troubled. It seems, however, that their facial expression when happy differs in some way from that used by the Japanese during this greeting. I found that it is very difficult for Americans to smile broadly before they are sure of their feelings about someone — and this cultural difference seems to be at least partially responsible for talk by Westerners about the enigmatic Oriental smile.

The Japanese do have facial expressions, but these are often subtle, delicate ones. Perhaps the often expressed sentiment that the Japanese lack facial expression is due to their not expressing their emotions so frankly and openly. And Westerners seem to have difficulty interpreting the subtle facial expressions of the Japanese.

Words of greeting united with action

After facial expression, the next problem for those students was the total timing of the greeting. There are certain prescribed movements which should accompany the words *hajimemashite*, *doozo yoroshiku*, or _____ *de gozaimasu*. The students came toward me as I moved toward them. At a set distance we stopped. According to Japanese custom, at that time one says *hajimemashite* while starting to bow. If one lacks confidence in this bowing movement, the expression *hajimemashite* will not come out smoothly either. Instead, the whole attempt will come out looking exactly like a Japanese child's bow, with the upper half of the body stiffly flopping forward and then quickly coming upright again and *hajimemashite* blurted out uncoordinated with the bow. These students had not yet mastered bowing, and it became only too clear to me that when students have mastered expressions in a foreign language with only their heads and mouths, they will be unable to use them naturally and with the proper accompanying behavior in real life.

Is it possible to learn to talk from tapes alone?

When I think about it, there are cases where the same thing happens to Japanese who study English exclusively from language tapes. They repeat over and over again the sounds of the words alone while ignoring the situation in which those words are said and the nonverbal behavior which is used with them. They lose their confidence entirely, therefore, when they find themselves in an actual English-speaking situation.

For example, once when I was returning from San Francisco to Japan I was asked to look after a Japanese who could not understand any English; we flew back together, and it turned out that he had been quite confident about his English before leaving Japan. He had purchased almost all the English-conversation tapes for sale in Tokyo and had practically memorized them so that he could say sentences as rapidly and as smoothly as on the tapes. He consequently boarded the airplane bound for the United States brimming over with confidence. But then when he arrived at the airport in San Francisco, he found that he could not understand the conversations being held around him or the questions of the immigration officers. Of course the content of those questions must have been on the tapes he had studied even though the wording was not exactly the same, but the wide gap between the model voices on his tapes and the actual voices of the officers at the San Francisco Airport was a great shock to him.

This story suggests that we must make a distinction between training for speaking and training for listening in foreign-language education. The major cause of this particular person's loss of confidence was his ignorance of how to respond in a real-life situation: his study did not prepare him to predict in what kind of place or situation, with what kind of facial expression, or even from what height he would hear spoken English. Unfortunately, he failed to regain his lost confidence during his several weeks in the United States, and he returned to Japan having spoken only a few words of English.

THE SITUATIONAL NATURE OF JAPANESE

The form of the answer is determined by the question

Consider the sentence, *Watakushi-wa Kyooto-e ikimashita* (I went to Kyoto). There is nothing wrong with it as a written sentence. But in what situation could one use this sentence in the spoken language?

If the question was, *Kyooto-e itta-kai* (Did [you] go to Kyoto?), the sense of the above sentence could, at its simplest, be expressed without any words at all but by simply nodding. It is also possible to confirm that one went to Kyoto by simply saying yes (*hai*). Or else one could add "I went" and say "Yes, I went" (*Hai, ikimashita*). Any of these responses adequately conveys the information that you went to Kyoto. Accordingly, *Watakushi-wa Kyooto-e ikimashita* would not emerge as a response to the question *Kyooto-e itta kai*.

What if the question were *Doko-e itta-no-ka* (Where did [you] go?)? In this case, the place name would appear in the answer: *Kyooto-e ikimashita* ([I] went to Kyoto); it is unlikely that one would say *Watakushi-wa Kyooto-e ikimashita*.

Watakushi-wa Kyooto-e ikimashita is possible as an answer, however, to the question, *Kimi-wa Kyooto-e itta-kai* (Did *you* go to Kyoto?), said with special emphasis on *kimi* (you) through its having higher prominence or being said stronger. This, then, is the first case in which this sentence is a possible response.

In this way, the sentence *Watakushi-wa Kyooto-e ikimashita* will not occur without a special context, and its content will usually be expressed in other forms. And another important point is that the form of the response is deeply related to the preceding sentence, in this case the question: the form of the response is determined by the content or form of the preceding sentences.

In the question *Kimi-wa Kyooto-e itta-kai* (Did you go to Kyoto?), *kimi* (you) and *Kyooto-e* (to Kyoto) are both specified. In this case, the most appropriate response omits both *kimi* and Kyoto. Or, in order to properly understand actual spoken Japanese, perhaps it is better to say that in this set of question and answer, *kimi* and *Kyooto* appear in the question alone and not in the answer. At any rate, it is only in special cases that *watakushi-wa* (I) will be included to form the sentence *Wata-*

kushi-wa Kyooto-e ikimashita; this form will be used when "you" (*kimi*) is being selected from all the other possible people, when you alone are being questioned about whether you went or not.

Native-speakers of English tend to carry over into Japanese the pattern used in English of rarely omitting the subject — although, of course, it is arguable how frequently complete sentences are said in English either. The main elements of the above sentence in English would be "I," "go," and "Kyoto," and English-speakers are likely to use these same elements in forming a Japanese sentence as well, replying to the various questions above with *Watakushi-wa Kyooto-e ikimashita*.

This pattern frequently turns up in the Japanese of foreign students. But if they should use *Watakushi-wa Kyooto-e ikimashita* in response to *Kimi, Kyooto-e ittakai*, the chances are that this will not be taken as a simple, straightforward answer but as one laying special emphasis on "me, myself," or as one calling the place, Kyoto, to the attention of the listener.

The importance of the situation for the form of the sentence

As I wrote earlier, one should consider this sentence — *Watakushi-wa Kyooto-e ikimashita* — as formed within the framework of one sentence in its particular context and, further, within the framework of a set of several connected sentences. This sentence demonstrates that the form of a given sentence is not set at the level of that sentence but that natural, good spoken sentences should be thought about in terms of the group of sentences we call a conversation.

In the previous section, I talked about this sentence as a response to a question. In the question prompting this answer too, the more explicit forms *Kimi, Kyooto-e itta-kai* or *Anata-wa Kyooto-e ikimashita-ka* will not usually appear; in most cases, words like *kimi* (you; familiar) and *anata* (you; polite) are not used. That omission is due to a reliance on the nonverbal situation, i.e., the listener being present right in front of the speaker.

We have also seen the important role played by the situation, the physical conditions surrounding the speech act, in both the choice of words and the form of the sentence, in the earlier discussion of *Ocha-o doozo nonde-kudasai.*

For example, say you are drinking beer. You would not usually say *"Biiru-o nomimasen-ka"* (Won't you have some beer?) when offering that beer to a friend. Rather, the standard way of saying that would be *"Nomimasen-ka"* (Won't you have [some]?). And if you should say *"Biiru-o nomu-kai"* (Will you have some beer?) even though the beer is right there in front of you, that will in effect be saying that other drinks are also possible and you have chosen beer from among them. In this situation, one does not usually use the word beer directly but instead says something like *"Doozo nonde-kudasai"* (Please drink [some]) or *"Ikaga-desu-ka"* (How about [some]?). Of course such expressions as *"Doozo biiru-o nonde-kudasai"* (Please drink the beer) or *"Biiru-wa ikaga-desu-ka"* (How about some beer?) are possible, but these variants occur when the speaker thinks the listener has some special attitude toward beer. These are not set expressions regularly used to offer beer to someone.

When the Japanese, thinking of this *"Ikaga-desu-ka"* (How about [some]?), omit the implied object and say in English "Would you care for?" or "Do you want to have?", the meaning is not immediately clear to the listener. Similarly, if they should offer a seat to an American guest who has just entered the room by saying "Please" alone — as *doozo* is used in Japanese

— there is a good possibility that the guest will be confused and not know what to do.

The use of *kore, sore, are, dore*

In discussing language use in relation to the physical situation, I am reminded of the functioning of *kore* (this), *sore* (that, it), *are* (that), and *dore* (which one), even though that may be thought of as a problem of vocabulary rather than sentence form.

Most Japanese have had little occasion to think about the difference in meaning of these four words, but they actually have a unique distribution of meaning among the group of words in the languages of the world called demonstratives. And they thus constitute one trouble point for foreigners learning Japanese.

Many Japanese are taught in junior high school that *kore* is equivalent to the English "this," *sore* to "it," and *are* to "that." However, these are not really equivalent, and the situation is more complicated than this: *sore* corresponds to "that," and *are* means "that" plus some extra meaning and functions similarly to "the." And since *kore*, *sore*, and *are* have different rules of usage from the demonstratives in their native languages, even foreigners who have attained considerable fluency in Japanese frequently have trouble with their usage.

When the demonstrative nouns *kore, sore, are*, and the corresponding demonstrative adjectives *kono, sono, ano* are used in relation to the nonverbal situation, we can roughly define their usage in the following way: *ko-* words are used to refer to things spatially close to the speaker or belonging to the speaker, *so-* words to refer to things close to the listener or belonging to the listener, and *a-* words to refer to things separate from both the speaker and the listener or in the state of being known to both of them.

Although of course these words are always bound by the rules of the nonverbal situation, there is also a usage determined by the verbal context: matters that have already appeared in the conversation are later referred to as *kore* or *sore*. The frequency of usage of this *kore* and *sore* in the spoken language is very high, and it is hard to imagine everyday conversation without *kore*, *sore*, or *are*.

Among the *ko-*, *so-*, and *a-* words used according to verbal context, *are* in particular is used in a way characteristic of the Japanese language. I said above that *are* is related to the situation and is used for things that are far from both the speaker and the listener or that can be recognized by both of them; when *are* is used in context, the latter condition becomes the major prerequisite. It is not difficult to think of concrete examples from everyday life.

For example, at home the Japanese often say *"Are-o motte-kite-kure"* (Bring me that, will you?) or at work *"Are, doo natta"* (How did that turn out?), to seek some action or ask about something. The sentence *Are-o motte-kite-kure* is built on the premise that the listener will know what the speaker is referring to by *are* and will thus be able to infer what the speaker wants brought.

Similarly, *Are, doo natta* presupposes that *are* will be understood by the listener as referring to something that the speaker and listener have talked about before, whether it be some business matter arising the day before that has to be seen to or whether it is some problem involving dealings with another party.

It is possible, of course, to spell out the matter involved instead of using this *are*, as in *Sakujitsu-no A shoosa-e-no baibai-keika-hookoku-wa doo natte-iru-ka* (What happend to the other day's report on transactions with the A trading company?) or *Sumanai-keredo, tabako-to haizara-o motte-kite-kure* (Excuse me, but could you bring me my cigarettes and an ashtray?). But generally speaking, rather than clearly indicating the thing or matter, the Japanese customarily carry on their conversations using *are*.

A clue to the fundamental nature of Japanese culture

This latter usage of *are* may be criticized as evidence that the way Japanese use their language is not precise or, on the contrary, it can be taken as evidence that the Japanese language is very convenient for conveying one's desires. In either case, no one can deny that words do exist in Japanese for cigarettes and ashtray or for the other day's documentation for transactions with the A trading company, and the fact that those matters do not have to be indicated directly but can simply be referred to as *are* allows us to make certain inferences about the particular nature of the Japanese use of language in everyday speech.

And this usage of *are* also provides fresh material for thinking about the nature of Japanese culture. Although one can discuss the characteristics of Japanese culture using such concrete and easily observable artifacts as buildings, paintings, and art works, examination of the spoken language gives special insight into the psychology of the Japanese, as can be seen in the use of *are*.

Chapter 3. The Special Characteristics of Spoken Japanese (1)

— What is said and to whom it is said —

WHAT IS AND IS NOT SAID

Is silence a virtue in Japan?

For the Japanese, the ideal form of communication seems to be that found in a close relationship where one's wishes can be conveyed by using *are* (that) or by subtle signs in one's facial expression and demeanor alone. This form of communication is often used in films and on television to show the closeness existing between two people, and the nonverbal, heart-to-heart (more literally, stomach-to-stomach!) communication called *haragei* impresses foreigners, who regard it as one important characteristic of Japanese behavior — but also criticize it for its possible ambiguity.

If we examine without preconception the actual language behavior of the Japanese, however, it is evident that there has been a sizable increase in the number of talkative individuals recently. Especially noticeable is the decrease of very reserved children and women, who were formerly seen and not heard in Japanese life. This change is reflected in the results of a little experiment I have done over the past ten years. When meeting students the first time that day, I ask *"Doo-datta"* (How was it?) right after exchanging greetings. I feel that their response has gradually changed. Recently more of them are confused about how to respond. Perhaps it is gradually becoming out of date to use *are* to avoid clearly asking "What?".

Is hemming and hawing a problem?

When Ohira Masayoshi was elected president of the Liberal-Democratic Party and became the prime minister of Japan, the mass media made much of his slow and fumbling speaking style. Letters to the editor also took up the problem of Ohira's hemming and hawing. Almost all of these comments were to the effect that the prime minister of Japan should speak more clearly and decisively. As far as I know, no one took the opposite position that, on the contrary, it could be good to have a taciturn prime minister. Rather, all felt that in this international age, a prime minister who habitually goes "eer. . ." or "uhh. . ." is a problem. However, the statements of those journalists and letter writers do not present a true picture of the attitude of the Japanese toward the spoken language. It is safe to say that a considerable percentage of the Japanese people find acceptable a somewhat slow or ambiguous speaking style. If Ohira had been a fluent and somewhat glib speaker, there would undoubtedly have been criticism of that too.

Not talking as a mark of adulthood

The Japanese have, on the whole, become more talkative, but at the same time the thinking is still strong that not saying things and not talking too much is a mark of adulthood.

The influence of this attitude can be seen, for example, in the language development of elementary school children. When visiting elementary and junior high schools, I have noticed that the children in the lower grades of elementary school are extremely positive and active about speaking in class and generally speak in loud voices. But in the upper grades of the same school, the children speak in small voices which are hard to hear, and their eagerness to speak has largely disappeared. Junior high and high school students seem to shrink from talking a lot even with their friends. This might be dismissed as a problem of those responsible for educating and counseling the young, but in actuality it is societal rules at operation within these groups of children and students that are acting to check their talking. While the attitude that silence is golden has weakened quite a bit in Japanese society, it is still difficult for someone who talks too much to be accepted into a group.

There is also a tendency in Japan to regard speaking in a voice which is not too loud and is not threatening in any way for one's listener as better than speaking in a loud, clear voice that can be easily understood by that listener. At funerals and wakes, in particular, little attention is paid to the content of one's remarks, and it is the custom to mumble so that they cannot be fully heard. This custom would seem to be rooted in more than simply the special nature of the occasion.

The Japanese fondness for speeches

It is often remarked that the Japanese are poor at public speaking, and it is rare to find the lively style seen among Americans and other foreigners in a Japanese speaker. I doubt if that is due to the Japanese not having the custom of speaking before others or simply being poor at speaking, however. The Japanese are actually quite fond of making speeches. At dinner parties and other gatherings the Japanese will often stand up one by one and give short talks. Many Americans living in Japan seem to have some trouble in giving these extemporaneous speeches — as do Japanese educated outside of Japan.

With the expansion of Japanese companies overseas have emerged growing numbers of Japanese children who have lived and been educated abroad. One teacher giving special classes to third graders who had just returned to Japan asked them to make a short speech about what they had done the weekend before. The students found this very difficult to do and refused; they said that in American schools the students do not ordinarily stand in front of everyone and give impromptu talks like this. While it is rare for Japanese students to push themselves forward to talk, if a teacher tells them to do so, they can stand in front of the other students and talk about what they have done or give their opinion about some subject. This cultivated ability stands them in good stead in making speeches at banquets and other occasions. All are somehow able to speak adequately, even though declaring all the while that the Japanese are poor at making speeches or that they have no confidence in their ability to speak. In family dramas on television, we often see someone agonizing over the prospect of making a speech or even going blank while giving a speech, but I personally have never seen a Japanese become flustered and unable to continue while making a speech.

The order of speaking at meetings

In any group that meets regularly in Japan, an order of who speaks first, second, and so on is soon established. In most cases, that order starts from the oldest person, the person with the highest status, or the most experienced person. In cases where the highest ranking, oldest, or most experienced person does not speak, it is difficult for the younger and less experienced persons to speak, and the conversation will lag. While this tendency is not completely absent in the case of Americans or other foreigners, on the whole the order of talking is free. Sometimes Japanese who have spent many years studying in the United States ignore the order described above and vigorously speak out at university faculty meetings in Japan. Then those around them will say, "Ah, you can always tell who's been trained in America."

A set order in the classroom

The order in which the teacher calls on students in the classroom also varies according to country. In Japanese schools, the teachers almost always follow the order students are listed in the attendance register, which is also the order of seating. In the United States, this method of teaching is criticized as leading to lazy students who only pay attention when their turn is coming. The Chinese, however, seem to follow a fixed order even more rigorously than the Japanese do. In my limited experience, Chinese students become completely disoriented if called on out of order.

Talkative or quiet according to the situation

We can see that it is dangerous to categorically label the Japanese as talkative or taciturn, since the degree to which a given person talks is determined by external conditions such as the order of speaking described above or the situation. For example, one man I know is viewed by everyone at work as very quiet, but at home with his family he is talking all the time. Other persons are the exact opposite: they talk vigorously at work and try hard to entertain people in social situations but hardly talk at all to their family or others in their immediate circle. When deciding whether the Japanese as a whole talk a lot or a little, one must consider at what time and with what people they talk a lot, in what situation they are silent, and about what subjects they talk a lot or are quiet.

WHO ONE DOES AND DOES NOT TALK TO

Greetings as confirmation

Greetings are a good source of data when one is trying to determine who speaks to whom. We can consider greetings as one stage in communication; in general, they are used to preserve or initiate social relations. But what specific meaning do greetings have in Japan?

For the Japanese, greetings are used not so much to create new human relationships as to protect and reaffirm already-established ones; they can be thought of as a means of mutually confirming that the other is still a friend. Greetings can have a different function for foreigners. For example, if you pass an American in the lobby of a hotel in a large Japanese city and your eyes should happen to meet, it will not be unusual if that American greets you. Or if you are facing each other in an elevator, a foreigner will probably say something to you and then make some greeting. But what will be the response of a Japanese to this greeting? Some Japanese might answer easily in Japanese or English, but most will probably avert their eyes and try to cover their embarrassment with a nervous smile.

This Japanese attitude toward strangers has also appeared in a debate in the newspaper letters to the editor section about giving up one's seat in the train. The letters complained that even when quite elderly persons are standing, those seated look away and pretend not to notice. If an acquaintance is standing, however, perhaps someone from work, they immediately stand up and offer their seat even if that person should happen to be a strong, healthy middle-aged man. The debate, centering over whether this attitude should be changed or not, demonstrated how strong this tendency is in Japanese life.

Greetings as a jogger

In the spring of 1977, I carried out a small investigation into the use of greetings at the request of the editor of a column in the Japanese-language *Yomiuri* newspaper entitled "On-the-spot Japanese" (*Nihongo no genba*).[3] In this investigation, I greeted people jogging around the Imperial Palace in Tokyo one morning to see what their response would be. This small-scale study was prompted by the widespread concern about how young Japanese no longer greet others even when meeting on a mountain path and about whether the Japanese might not have forgotten how to properly greet others. Before we carried out this experiment, the newspaper people and I had differing expectations about the outcome. The newspaper people felt that the percentage of people *not* responding would be a little higher whereas I felt that, at least as far as joggers were concerned, the opposite would be the case.

The morning we went out to do the experiment was a nice, fresh morning with the cherry trees along the jogging route on the verge of coming into full bloom. The joggers were running counterclockwise around the Palace, and we ran in the opposite direction so that we would be facing them on the path. First I came jogging along in a running suit with a towel draped around my neck. A little way behind me came newspaper men also in running outfits with note pads and a tape recorder. Their role was to record the response when I called out "Good morning" (*Ohayoo-gozaimasu*) to the person running toward me.

The results are shown in Tables 1 and 2. Almost all of the forty-odd people I greeted responded. I myself secretly felt some moments of doubt that these people running and panting for breath might be too occupied to answer, but all but two of them responded to me in one way or other — with *Ohayoo, Ohayoo-gozaimasu* (Good morning), *Osu* (Hiya; used by men to men), or *Oo* (slightly rougher than *Osu*). The two exceptions were actually due to poor timing of my greeting, and with better timing there probably would have been a 100 percent response rate. As far as these figures alone are concerned, my predictions were accurate.

Table 1. Responses of Joggers

Ohayoo-gozaimasu	5
Ohayossu, ohayoosu, oosu, osu	19
Yaa, haa, yo	3
foreign language	1
lowering head	10
raising hand	2
no response	2
TOTAL	42

Table 2. Responses of Ordinary Passers-by

Ohayoo-gozaimasu	2
Ohayossu	1
lowering head	4
smile	4
no response	15
TOTAL	26

However, there was one more interesting result. While running along, I also greeted the people walking by in the same way with *Ohayoo-gozaimasu*. These people were almost all dressed in suits, some walking singly and some in groups. The results, shown in Table 2, are almost the complete opposite of those for the joggers. That is, the response rate was less than 50 percent, and few of those responding gave me a complete greeting. A number of these walkers looked at me suspiciously, as if wondering what ulterior motive I might have in greeting them.

Insiders and outsiders

It is clear from these results that being dressed and perceived as one of the group of joggers was a large factor in the exchange of greetings. For those in suits, I was an outsider having no reason to speak to them. For the joggers, on the other hand, I was perceived as being one of their group and greeted as such even while they were engaged in strenuous activity.

As the underlying motivation behind greetings for the Japanese is making this insider-outsider distinction, they use greetings to heighten group-consciousness or to confirm their membership in the group, and they do not customarily greet those outside their group. Consequently, it is only natural that talking to strangers in elevators, hotel lobbies, parks, or the like does not normally take place among the Japanese.

The risk of misunderstanding is thus ever present when the Japanese interact with foreigners, since the latter lack this insider-outsider framework guiding their perceptions and actions toward others and find it difficult to understand. Even if a Japanese has only the best of intentions toward a foreigner, as long as those thoughts are not put into words as a greeting, they may not be understood as such. Although the Japanese may try to convey their feelings through facial expression, a foreigner may well find it difficult to judge from the smile of a Japanese what his or her real feelings are inside, even if that expression is readily understandable to another Japanese. One's good will can be conveyed through one's actions. The Japanese tendency to act based on this insider-outsider distinction, however, can sometimes result in lamentable behavior.

Attacking outsiders=strengthening group solidarity

I witnessed the following behavior in Auckland, New Zealand, seven or eight years ago. Some Japanese, apparently members of a tour group, were shopping in a souvenir shop near the lobby of the hotel. When they had made their selections, they took them to the clerk, a conscientious-looking young woman of Maori descent. She started adding up the purchases but became somewhat flustered and was not able to reach a price for all those articles right away. Then the Japanese started complaining to each other: "That's an old machine she's using," "She's slow at figures, isn't she," "That's a poor way to run a business."

Thinking she would not be able to understand Japanese, they unabashedly complained in front of that young clerk. She continued to add up the figures without any change of expression, but she could undoubtedly tell from their faces that they were not saying anything good about her or the shop. At that time it was no longer safe to assume that a foreigner would have no knowledge of Japanese, but what bothered me even more was the clear motive behind that complaining: the heightening of group consciousness and the strengthening of one's own ties to the group through criticism of an outsider. That was truly an unpleasant sight to see.

This sort of scene can often be observed among the Japanese in Japan as well. By belittling a third person outside of the group, one heightens insider solidarity and also reassures oneself of one's position as an insider. One can often observe the Japanese trying to preserve their status and position in this way. And the setting up of boundaries and finally feeling safe if one is inside those boundaries is tied to the impersonal, and occasionally inhuman, treatment of those outside the boundaries. It also leads to an emphasis on preserving harmonious relations within the group and a de-emphasis on establishing a firm sense of self and a respect for the individual. This pattern of behavior is one major cause of the often expressed criticism that the

Japanese are very strong in groups, but individually cannot express any clear opinions and have no idea of what they want to do.

Dakaraa, bokutachi-waa . . .
As we have seen, one cannot categorically say that the Japanese are poor at talking, since whether an individual will talk a lot or hardly at all is determined by to whom he or she is speaking. Many Japanese are very talkative within their own group but find it difficult to talk with strangers in a public place.

Recently the speaking style of young people has been receiving much popular attention in Japan. One mark of that style is to pronounce one part of the phrases at the end of a sentence or clause higher, lengthening the particle, as in ___ *-dee*, ___ *-waa*, or ___ *-gaa*, and with the following part of the utterance spoken lower. This intonation pattern is not used at all times and places; it does not appear, for example, when young people are relaxed and talking together in a coffee shop. But the same persons will display this pattern when they are approached by strangers and when they must answer their questions or explain something; it will also be found when they are questioned closely by an acquaintance. Even though it is easy for them to talk with people they know, they seem to be at a loss for words when they have to talk with complete strangers or people they do not know well.

WHO ONE TALKS TO AND WHY

The Japanese-foreigner distinction
One major boundary that the Japanese draw when they speak is that between Japanese and foreigner. This boundary is based not on nationality but on appearance, that is, on whether one looks Japanese or not.

Two Americans doing research at a Japanese university personally experienced this distinction. One of them was white and quite advanced in Japanese. He could handle everyday conversation without any problems and also read specialized works and give simple speeches in Japanese. The other was a third-generation Japanese-American who had hardly studied Japanese at all and could only understand common greetings and the like. One day these two went to a department store to do some shopping. They wanted to buy some tea cups and coffee cups. Therefore the white student asked a clerk, *"Koohii-no chawan-o misete-hoshii-ga"* (We would like to see some coffee cups). But even though the white student had asked the question, the clerk directed her answer to the Japanese-American student, telling him *"Koohii-jawan-wa achira-ni gozaimasu"* (The coffee cups are over there).

The Japanese-American, naturally enough, did not understand anything she had said and looked helplessly at the other student for help. The white student then asked the clerk, *"Aa, soo-desu-ka. Sore-dewa koocha-no chawan-mo onaji tokoro-ni arimasu-ka"* (Oh, I see. And are Western tea cups in the same place?). The clerk once again directed her response to the Japanese-American, *"Koocha-no chawan-wa sono mukoogawa-ni narande-orimasu"* (The teacups are found past the coffee cups).

One can often see similar examples of not responding directly to white foreigners even after they have said something in Japanese. I sometimes escort leading foreign specialists in Japanese studies to Japanese government offices, and here too the pattern of conversation is remarkably like the above department store episode. If the discussions are in Japanese, the officials invariably avoid talking directly to these foreigners, and instead direct their remarks to me, a Japanese standing or sitting near the Americans. Even though it would make more sense to ask those American specialists responsible for the programs, they will ask me something like, *"Amerika-dewa ittai dono yoo-ni shite Nihon-kenkyuu-no gakusei-o yoosei-shite-iru-no-ka"* (How are they training Japanologists in the United States?).

This phenomenon is by no means limited to department stores or government offices. When white students learning Japanese inquire of someone on a station platform or inside a train, *"Kono densha-wa doko-yuki-desu-ka"* (Where is this train going?), often those Japanese will just shake their heads or wave their hands in front of their faces in a gesture of incomprehension and say, *"Yoku wakarimasen"* (I don't understand). The student, thinking his or her poor Japanese is at fault, will ask the question again, saying it more carefully. But even though their Japanese is correct and there is no reason for it not to be understood, those Japanese will still fail to understand it.

In fact, many Japanese have the preconception that anything coming out of a white foreigner's mouth is English or some other foreign language that they cannot understand. Even if those foreigners should be speaking Japanese, they will deny this fact because they think a foreigner cannot possibly be speaking Japanese.

The ordeal for foreigners of Japanese descent

On the other hand, as seen in the department store example above, a different ordeal is in store for those foreigners or Japanese nationals who look Japanese but do not speak Japanese. Most members of the third and fourth generations of foreign nationals of Japanese descent have not studied Japanese; even those with some knowledge of Japanese do not always speak it well since they did not grow up in a Japanese-speaking environment. They have usually studied Japanese as a foreign language in college and then come to Japan to study further. They come to Japan with many expectations and hopes; they feel a complex affection and yearning toward Japan, the land of their grandparents. Unhappily, however, these feelings have almost always been effectively destroyed a few months after their arrival.

One third-generation Japanese-American graduate student came to me very upset. He had gone on a trip to Nagano Prefecture and stayed overnight at a *ryokan*. The group in the room next to his was quite noisy, and he went to ask them to be a little more quiet.

He seems to have said something like *"Onegai-desu-kara, shizuka-ni shite-kudasai"* (I'd like to ask you to please be quiet). However, they just made fun of his still less than perfect Japanese, saying *"Omae-wa ittai doko-kara kita-n-da. Henna shaberikata-o suru yatsu-da-na"* (Where did you come from? You really talk funny), and did not pay any attention to what he was trying to say.

Good service for English-speakers

On the other hand, we frequently encounter this kind of story. In an article somewhere, a foreigner revealed that he made it a practice never to speak Japanese when he was staying at a hotel since the bellboys and other employees gave him much better service if he spoke in English. It appears that even thirty years after the end of World War II, the Japanese have not lost their complex toward Westerners.

These examples all show that the Japanese have a different attitude and pattern of response toward whites and non-whites. Their attitude is completely different — usually for the worse — not only toward foreigners of

Japanese descent but also toward exchange students from China and Southeast Asia.

The Seven Samurai and *The Magnificent Seven*

We have seen that in Japan the way of talking changes depending on to whom one is speaking and on the time and purpose of that talking. We have also seen the importance of the attitude toward talking itself.

Some differences in the Japanese and American attitudes toward speech can be seen in two films, *The Seven Samurai* and *The Magnificent Seven*. *The Seven Samurai*, a masterpiece made by the film director Kurosawa Akira, was later adapted as the American film *The Magnificent Seven*. When I saw these two films, I was surprised at the differences and similarities between them. Minor differences existed in the characters and background of the incident, such as the use of sword or pistol and spear or knife, but the development of the story itself — outsiders coming to the aid of suffering villagers — was almost identical. One place, however, was completely different in the two films.

In *The Seven Samurai*, the villagers gather under the command of the seven samurai to fight mountain bandits. The bandits attack the village and fierce fighting ensues. The seven samurai emerge from their hiding places and fall on the bandits. In the end, the bandit attack is successfully repulsed. It was the beginning of this scene that was completely different in *The Magnificent Seven*. There the bandits do not attack in one swoop, with the waiting seven immediately coming out and returning their attack. Instead, the attackers and defenders face each other at the entrance to the town in a momentary truce. One of the defenders asks, "So you want to fight?", and the fighting starts after that.

It is my guess that most Japanese would not find

anything strange or blameworthy about the samurai attack on the bandits in *The Seven Samurai*. They would, however, have doubts about both sides talking together before starting to fight, as in the American version; it would be difficult to convince them of the necessity of two groups ready to kill each other first carrying out discussions with each other. Since the adaptation follows the original faithfully except for this one scene, we must regard this change as significant.

We can conclude — without becoming involved in their relative merits — that a wide gap exists between the expectations toward and value placed on talking of the Japanese and the Americans. Memories of World War II seem to have been pushed aside for the sake of good relations today between the United States and Japan, but these differing attitudes toward speech may well be related to the problem of the Japanese attack on Pearl Harbor: it is clear that, at the very least, the Japanese and Americans hold different attitudes toward a declaration of war.

THE LANGUAGE BEHAVIOR OF AN AVERAGE JAPANESE, MR. J

The attitude toward persuasion

For what purpose do the Japanese use words? We could say that their motive is to transmit information to others, but this statement is very vague and superficial. We must specify what kind of information that is — whether concerned with a certain incident or factual matter or with the speaker's emotions, opinions, or judgments — and what form that transmission of information takes. And although it is true that the purpose of conversation is roughly the same for any people anywhere in the world, here we are focusing our discussion on the differences.

In order to illustrate the special characteristics of talking and using words in Japanese, I would like to postulate an average Japanese speaker, Mr. J, and examine his language behavior. Let's make Mr. J a typical white-collar worker in his 40s. There is nothing particularly conspicuous about his language behavior. He looks through the newspaper every day and reads books and magazines regularly. He is by no means lacking or handicapped in his language use toward others and himself feels that he is active about speaking at meetings and is not particularly poor at speaking. Although he has some difficulties with the formal intricacies of Japanese letter-writing and occasionally abandons writing a letter, he conscientiously performs his duties at work and writes any necessary letters or other materials.

Mr. J does sometimes feel dissatisfied with his spoken language skills. For example, he feels that he is very poor at persuasion. More accurately, this is something he dislikes. Somewhere in the back of his mind is still embedded the idea that persuading others is not of high value — perhaps it is something that should not be done at all. He feels a strong antipathy toward using words to convince others of some matter and cause them to act in accordance with his will. He thus dislikes persuading others no matter who they may be — those above or below him in age, experience, or position as well as outsiders or members of his family. Although he could probably persuade someone if he had to, he will avoid doing so. If, for example, his children should take some stand against him, he will not actively try to persuade them. When Mr. J does find himself in a position where he has to persuade others, he feels very disgruntled and uncomfortable. He can accept the necessity for persuasion in certain limited instances toward his superiors at work, but in general he finds it unpleasant and distasteful. While it is not so hard for him to tell someone at work how a certain job should be done, he has not once tried to convince his boss to raise his salary, even when he felt dissatisfied with it. Of course he has hinted to him that he could not manage on his present salary. But even though this hinting had no direct results, he was not moved to come right out and ask for a raise.

'Please give me a raise'

Generally speaking, the Japanese find it very difficult to use words to attempt to persuade their superiors to raise their salaries. This stance is a cause of friction when Japanese and Americans or other foreigners are working together. The Japanese employees may grumble together about how unhappy they are with their wages, but they will hesitate to go directly to their American superior and ask for a raise. When they do finally request a raise, their discontent has been bottled up for so long that the negotiations become quite heated. Then the American boss wonders why they didn't just come and talk to him earlier. One can accuse the superior of a lack of insight for not sensing their dissatisfaction, but there is a considerable gulf between the behavior used in the two cultures to express dissatisfaction. And this gulf exists for the attitude toward the written language as well.

Meticulous at work, easygoing at home

To return to Mr. J once again, he handles paperwork at the office very meticulously. He never skips lines in letters or other materials from outside the company or in paperwork forwarded to him from within the company. He scrutinizes each word and phrase, having certain parts rewritten as necessary. However, in his life outside the office, Mr. J does not show much interest in written materials such as contracts for purchases, gas, electricity, and so on. He does not usually look at these himself but entrusts them to his family. If he is shown papers by the other party to an agreement, he glances through them for courtesy's sake and stamps them with his seal without the thorough scrutinizing he gives papers at the office.

The Japanese attitude toward the law written down in words is an interesting question since in their everyday lives they do not carefully examine or place much value on contracts and the like. When American students in Japan rent a room, they may take two or three hours reading the contract they are given to sign. The landlord and intermediary are often somewhat put out by this behavior as the Japanese generally do not investigate the contents of written materials like contracts all that thoroughly.

The attitude toward debate

Mr. J dislikes debating or arguing as well as persuasion. More precisely, he does not mind debate or argument as long as it will not affect his interests or reputation or those of the other party if that debate should become heated. If, however, there is a possibility that he will be put at a disadvantage or will hurt the other, the edge of debate will inevitably be blunted. The Japanese try to evade thoroughgoing arguments that exhaustively investigate the rights and wrongs of a matter.

By definition, debate involves give-and-take. Mr. J, however, is not particularly skilled at thinking out his responses beforehand, deciding how he would answer if the other said such and such or trying to lay the groundwork for saying such and such. Rather, he fears a waste of time and possible damage to the human relationships involved. Consequently, while debate is accepted to a certain degree at meetings of persons close to one, if outsiders will be present, the Japanese think about ways to turn them into insiders rather than of ways to carry on the debate in words and thereby achieve certain results. Before a meeting takes place, the Japanese devote themselves to *nemawashi*, or laying the groundwork for obtaining their objectives (literally, digging around the roots of a tree before replanting). In order to achieve the desired results from a meeting, Mr. J believes that one should first meet privately with the persons who will be attending the meeting and talk with them about their opinions in order to be able to be 80-90 percent sure of what responses will be made at the meeting itself.

For this reason, the talk at the meeting is formalized; one can say that it all goes according to the predictions of Mr. J or, rather, that for Mr. J and almost all of the other participants, the function of the meeting is simply to confirm each other's intentions and wishes through putting into words what is already understood. All will return home satisfied with that. Someone may complain that the meeting had no real content, but no one will declare that they should never have another meeting like that one.

Topics in conversations with outsiders

Mr. J's weakness in talking with others in order to have them do something for him is connected with not having many topics of conversation at his disposal. Broadly speaking, he does not customarily make an effort to use words to introduce or grasp new topics, as can be seen in the case of the above meeting where all concerned carefully laid the groundwork beforehand. Therefore, he is always at a loss as to what to talk about when he meets strangers. On the occasions when he has been delegated to meet foreign visitors, he has given much thought to what to say but has never been able to think of any really good topics. As a result, he always ends up asking them something like "When did you come to Japan?", "What do you think of Japan?", or "How do you like *tempura* and *sashimi*?".

Foreigners do not particularly mind these sorts of questions the first two or three times, but tend to lose patience with them after ten days or so. They begin to feel a new interest in this phenomenon as a characteristic of Japanese culture after being asked the same questions over and over again for half a year. The foreigners then simply wait for their turn to speak, making allowances for the poor conversational skills of the Japanese with long-suffering expressions on their faces.

But however much we may deplore the unskilled Japanese handling of conversation with foreigners, this is very difficult to improve because there is no custom of preparing topics for conversation in everyday life. This situation gives rise to the risk of misunderstanding by foreigners at meetings and the like. At a Japanese meeting, whether of insiders or a more formal one including some outsiders, it is not regarded as especially bad form if a person remains completely silent. Of course if a good talker is present it will help things along, but if Mr. J were simply present, smiling and drinking tea, for two hours without saying a single word, he would not be criticized by his colleagues. But if he did the same thing at a meeting conducted by Americans, they would conclude that he was unhappy in some way with the people there or with the matter under discussion.

Complaining and foreigners

It is often very painful for the Japanese to tell someone something or to appeal to them for something. There is also a problematical conversational gambit that the Japanese will sometimes use when they are searching desperately for some topic or when, on the contrary, they are feeling fairly at ease: idle complaining. Many foreigners seem to have some trouble knowing how to deal with this complaining by the Japanese. Mr. J himself does not complain so much, but his wife once had a bad experience with that. When they were living for an extended period in Hawaii, she once complained quite a bit about him at a neighborhood gathering: "He's always busy with his job and he neglects me. He doesn't even talk to the children." (*Shigoto-ni isogashikute nakanaka kamatte-kurenai. Kodomotachi-tomo hanashi-o shite-kurenai.*) If she had said this at a gathering of Japanese, her listeners would have thought that she was asking if it was the same for them, if their husbands were busy too. Or perhaps, more cynically, they would have concluded that she was complaining to offer a topic of conversation, hiding her good family relationships out of consideration for the others. However, in Hawaii, the interpretation given her remarks was quite different. After the meeting had ended, she received many telephone calls offering to introduce her to a new man or to a lawyer! Other Japanese understand that when one is complaining about one's family or those around one, those remarks are usually not meant to be taken literally, but foreigners do not.

Japanese white-collar workers are fond of going out drinking together after work, and their conversation at that time is for the most part made up of this sort of complaining. One may well ponder what function this complaining plays for the Japanese.

Instruction in a more logical form of expression

We can imagine that when there is no general custom of talking to strangers, there may well be major weaknesses in speech, explanation, and description as well. It is possible, for instance, that there will be no custom of expressing factual relationships logically or of expressing matters in a rigorous matter, searching for logical connections between them. In fact, in Mr. J's experience, it is no easy matter to write a letter that is direct and to the point. At times it is necessary for him to write business letters to foreign countries. He writes these first in Japanese and they are then translated into English, but the English version is almost always less than half as long as the Japanese one. Disregarding matters of sentence form and grammar, the problem generally turns out to be the content of the explanation of the situation, the order of the words in that explanation, and repetition in the text.

Although Mr. J has himself felt the insufficiency of his language skills at times in his everyday life, he has never once made a real effort to become better at explaining things to people or received such training from others. He does not remember primary school so well, but he remembers his high school and college years quite clearly and has no memory of ever receiving any instruction in expressing a matter precisely and exactly. At work his superiors have said things like "How about saying this a little more clearly?" (*Moo sukoshi hakkiri ittara doo-ka*) or "Please explain this so it will be clearly understood" (*Chanto tsutawaru yoo-ni setsumei-shite-kure*), but no one has ever instructed him, "In this case it would be more suitable to explain it like this" (*Kono baai-wa kono yoo-ni setsumei-suru-no-ga yori tekisetsu-de aru*).

In addition to his not receiving this sort of positive guidance, he has been at the same time continually exposed to the negative influence of the strongly-rooted way of thinking surrounding him shown in "They ought to understand even if we don't put this into words"

(*Iwanakute-mo wakaru-daroo*) or "They'll understand when they see it" (*Mireba wakaru-daroo*). Mr. J wonders if that attitude of relying on people's understanding hasn't sometime or other rubbed off on him so that he has become lazy about trying to express things in words. He graduated from the humanities division of his university and always thought that those from the sciences division were probably more skilled at expressing and describing things logically, but recently he has heard that the weakness of expression in science education has become the subject of investigation and controversy. The science texts presently used in elementary and junior high schools in Japan apparently do not always have suitable texts.

Emotion also not expressed frankly

Much attention has been paid to the weakness of logical expression in the language behavior of the Japanese. It is said that the Japanese do not have the custom of explaining and expressing matters precisely and to the point. There is certainly some truth in this characterization, and Mr. J himself feels deeply the difficulty of producing explanatory sentences displaying a power of expression. While admitting problems in the precise expression of factual matters, many have praised Japanese for its richness in the expression of emotion. Actually, however, there seem to be problems in that area as well.

Certainly while Mr. J is reading along, he enjoys reading between the lines where much is left to the imagination more than paying attention to the precision of the descriptions; he is attracted by the nuances of the emotions hinted at there. However, when we think about the expression of emotion outside of literature, in everyday life, we run into problems. In fact a Chinese,

Mr. C, once told Mr. J that the Japanese are poor at openheartedly expressing their emotions, or rather, that they do not even try to do so. When Mr. J asked him why he said that, Mr. C replied that one example would be quarrels between husbands and wives in Japan; he was never sure if they were fighting or not. Fights in China between husband and wife or others are done with the two looking directly at each other and attacking each other in raised voices. But Japanese fights did not seem to be like that. Then Mr. J recalled a Japanese TV drama entitled *Fuufu* (A married couple). In one scene in that drama, the couple talked about separating but that scene did not look like an argument; there was no sharp exchange of words. Even though the content of that exchange was extremely bitter, it did not take the form of them yelling at each other. In a typical style of argument in Japan, the couple quarreled with their faces turned away from each other and with their words tightly controlled as well, using the polite honorific language. An American also said that he found that totally incomprehensible.

Is the antithesis of being poor in logical expression being strong in the expression of emotion? Being poor at expressing emotion frankly and suppressing emotion also are characteristic of Japanese language behavior. Our average Japanese Mr. J has problems in explaining things so that his opinions and evaluations will be easily understandable to his listeners, in his use of words to persuade others and cause them to take action, and in giving voice to his emotions. We will not concern ourselves here with whether that has a special value or not. At any rate, one cannot say that there are certain special characteristics in the way of talking of the Japanese that make Japanese superior to other languages.

Low expectations toward words

For what purpose do the Japanese use words and talk? It does not seem to be to express self-satisfaction or evade anxiety, to give themselves courage or rouse themselves to action. Does language then play a negative function for the Japanese? Do they use words to avoid the worsening of human relations, to avoid friction or conflict, to avoid misunderstandings? The Japanese do not offer theories deciding the ultimate rights and wrongs of a question. Nor do they use words to persuade others. However, as is indicated by the existence of the special respect language, there is an extremely strong attitude of consideration toward others and concern about what they are thinking. The Japanese seem to be speaking so as not to collide with each other, to be using words as a sort of quiet warning system.

At the very least, the philosophy underlying the Japanese expectations toward words is definitely not "What is unsaid will not be understood" (*iwaneba wakaranu*). Rather there seems to be a distrust, with little hope placed on language — or at least the spoken language — as evidenced in such sentiments as "It should be understood without putting it into words" or "It's something that can't be understood even if put into words."

Certainly the Japanese learn various things through words. Through them they have studied the legacy left by their ancestors and the fruits of the accumulated technology and research of the advanced Western nations. It seems, however, that they have yet to produce and give forth anything based on what they have ingested. One can say that language has become a means of acquisition for the Japanese, but not of creation. That may lead to thinking of language itself as something authoritative, or valuing what some authoritative figure has written or said. A language must be used to create or to make people act to be called a living language. In that sense, I wonder if we can say that the Japanese have made the Japanese language into a fully vital and vigorous instrument for thought and action.

Chapter 4. The Special Characteristics of Spoken Japanese (2)

— The tendency toward harmony and unity —

A WAY OF SPEAKING REQUIRING TWO PEOPLE

Giving *aizuchi*

A conversation or dialogue involves two persons, a speaker and a listener, except for special cases where one person is addressing a large number of people, such as television and radio shows, lectures, and speeches. In everyday conversation, one person speaks and then the other responds to that person's questions and gives his or her opinions in response to the first person's opinions. Then the first person listens to that response and says something else. In other words, we can say that a conversation or dialogue is created by a speaker and a listener, and words are exchanged like balls in a ping-pong game.

Although this pattern is regarded as a universal one, in fact it is not; the Japanese do not carry on a conversation in quite this way. Thus, when I was staying at a hotel in Hong Kong, I could tell at a glance which of a dozen or so groups of people chatting in the lobby were Japanese. The Japanese and Chinese are not so different from each other physically, but look quite different when talking in groups. More specifically, the Japanese give each other *aizuchi*, agreeable responses that make a conversation go smoothly (literally, alternate hammering by two blacksmiths). These *aizuchi* are not so frequent in serious conversations but are quite prominent in relaxed ones, and, although some Japanese may give fewer *aizuchi* than others, all Japanese give *aizuchi* while listening to their companions talk. These *aizuchi* are constantly employed in everyday life in Japan, a distinctive form of language behavior little seen elsewhere.

What exactly are these *aizuchi*? *Aizuchi* are spoken affirmatives such as *hai* (yes), *ee* (yes; informal), *haa* (yes; formal), *soo* (That's right), *soo-da soo-da* (That's it, that's it exactly), and *naruhodo nee* (Indeed!), as well as nonverbal affirmatives like nodding.

Aizuchi seem quite strange to foreigners at first. English-speakers studying Japanese often complain about the Japanese habit of breaking in on them while they are still talking. The Japanese, however, do not feel they are interrupting or interfering with the speaker when they give *aizuchi*. On the contrary, they feel aided by *aizuchi*; when they do not have much confidence, they are encouraged by their listener's *aizuchi* and thereby gain the confidence to continue talking. For speeches and lectures as well, the *aizuchi* of the audience or students give the speaker a yardstick as to how well the talk is going.

The giving of *aizuchi*, however, does not mean that the listener really understands or agrees with the content of an utterance. For instance, *hai* (yes) used as an *aizuchi* is sometimes identified by the Japanese with the English "yes," leading to problems when they use "yes" in English as they would *hai* in Japanese. Americans and Englishmen angrily say that the Japanese keep saying "yes, yes," but afterward it turns out that they do not really agree; they feel it impossible to understand their real intentions. This misunderstanding occurs because *hai* and "yes" are not completely equivalent to each other: the Japanese use of *hai* as an *aizuchi* does not by any means indicate that the listener is agreeing with what the speaker is saying. It is no more than a signal recognizing that the speaker is saying something and urging him or her to continue; it means, "Yes, I'm listening to what you're saying. Go on."

Similarly, a student may have given many *aizuchi* in class, but from his exam paper later it is evident that he had no understanding at all of the lectures. Thus spoken *aizuchi* or nodding are not exactly equivalent to "yes," and they do not mean that the listener has understood what is said or is agreeing with it.

Conversation as a joint production

Japanese conversation, as stated above, does not follow the common pattern of one person giving an opinion with the other person listening to that communication and then giving a new opinion or expressing some feeling; rather, a conversation is thought to be created together by two persons. It is even possible to speak with an intonation calling for *aizuchi* from the other person after a single word. For instance, if one says *sore-wa-ne* (literally, that is . . . .) with a particular intonation of the *ne*, the listener will have to respond with *un* (yeah, uh huh), *ee* (yes), or the like. Of course, not all Japanese-speakers favor this style of speech calling for many *aizuchi*, but conversation in Japan, especially everyday conversation, is characterized by the frequent use of *aizuchi*. This frequency is due to the rule requiring a response to even a single short word such as *boku-wa* . . . (I . . .).

This style of conversation makes talking on the telephone in Japanese very difficult even for foreigners quite advanced in their study of Japanese. They often feel somewhat out of step, as in the following all-too-possible telephone conversation.

    Japanese: *Moshi moshi.* (Hello.)
    Foreigner: *Moshi moshi.* (Hello.)
    Japanese: *Ee, kochira, anoo, Yamamoto-desu-ga.*

>   (Uuh, this is, err, Yamamoto.)
> Foreigner: . . . . .
> Japanese: *Moshi moshi.* (Are you there?)
> Foreigner: *Moshi moshi.* (Hello.)
> Japanese: *Kochira, Yamamoto-desu-ga, Jonson-san-wa* . . . (This is Yamamoto. Is Mr./Ms. Johnson . . .)
> Foreigner: . . . . .
> Japanese: *Moshi moshi.* (Are you there?)

The caller has identified himself as Yamamoto and held the *ga* of *Yamamoto-desu-ga* with a flat, extended tone to indicate his expectation of the listener giving an *aizuchi* like *hai*, *ee*, *haa* or the like. But the foreigner feels the sentence is unfinished and waits for Mr. Yamamoto to go on. When there is no response, the Japanese becomes worried and says *moshi moshi* to make sure the other is still on the line. The foreigner responds with *moshi moshi*. The Japanese then goes on and says "*Kochira, Yamamoto-desu-ga, Jonson-san wa* . . ." and waits for a response. This *Jonson-san-wa* is only the beginning of the sentence so the foreigner makes no response. It is this kind of conversation in which the Japanese person seems to be continually saying *moshi moshi* that discourages foreign students of Japanese and causes them to complain about how hard it is to talk on the telephone.

Viewed from another angle, this difficulty felt by foreigners provides further evidence that this is one of the special characteristics of Japanese conversation. That is, a conversation in Japanese is supported by the constant demonstration of the desire to continue it of both of the persons involved, and is a joint creation of these two persons.

The *aizuchi hai*

As mentioned above, this custom of giving *aizuchi*

leads Japanese-speakers to do the same in English. They tend to simply replace the *hai* used as *aizuchi* with "yes," resulting in a strange conversational style: when an American says something like "Tokyo is a big city . . ." and happens to pause momentarily, a Japanese will often say "yes, yes," saying "yes" two or three times as *hai* is often repeated when used as an *aizuchi*. All Japanese can sympathize with the desire to do this even though that way of speaking seems intrusive in English. In fact, it is not seen in Chinese either and seems to be found elsewhere only in Korea. The Korean 네 (nei) and 예 (yei) correspond to the Japanese *hai* and are used in the same way.

Father W. A. Grootaers has pointed out another implication of using *aizuchi*. He notes that international telephone calls in Japanese are very expensive. That is, the use of *aizuchi* lengthens the conversation and thereby increases the charge.

One sentence produced by two or more persons

Aizuchi are given in response to signals from the speaker, and the listener may also be prompted to add even more according to the intonation used. For example, when the speaker says, *"Ano, boku-wa-ne, kinoo Kyooto-e. . ."* (literally, Say, yesterday I to Kyoto . . .), the listener may well complete the sentence by saying *"itta-n-deshoo"* (literally, you probably went); this in effect forms the sentence *Boku-wa kinoo Kyooto-e itta* (I went to Kyoto yesterday). This pattern of conversation is seen quite often in Japanese.

At its extreme, two people may take turns and produce a sentence in three parts:

    A: *Boku-wa, kinoo-ne, Kyooto-e* (literally, I yesterday, to Kyoto)
    B: *Itta-n-ja nai-ka* (literally, you went, didn't you?)

A: *to omou-deshoo* (literally, you probably think so).

This would be impossible in English. A sentence is commonly thought of as one unit in an utterance by one person, but in Japanese, as we have seen here, two people can take part in making a sentence. In fact, it is not impossible to conceive of three or more persons participating; it is necessary to revise our way of thinking about the sentence, at least as far as spoken Japanese is concerned.

This way of producing sentences and conducting conversations is one major characteristic of spoken Japanese. We may well wonder what effect this language pattern has on the Japanese when they try to express something in a logical way or to state something in a monologue. Another relevant question is what possible interference this psychological attitude may produce when the Japanese are using a foreign language. At any rate, it is clear that this special characteristic of the listener anticipating the rest of the speaker's sentence before it is finished and giving *aizuchi* such as *hai* constitutes one clue for investigating the special nature of spoken Japanese.

A FORM OF EXPRESSION
WHICH AVOIDS OPPOSING OTHERS

English as tennis and Japanese as volleyball

In English and many other languages, the roles of speaker and listener are clearly differentiated and can even be regarded as being antagonistic to each other. But Japanese seems to be based on completely different principles; conversation in Japanese is not a give-and-take or confrontation between a speaker and listener having clearly-defined standpoints.

English conversation can be compared to ping-pong

or tennis. It has a give-and-take of words in which the two persons are like opponents, with one hitting the ball and the other waiting to hit it back. The speaker talks and the listener listens silently. Only when the ball comes flying to his or her side does the listener in turn become the speaker and return the ball.

We can think of Japanese conversation, however, as being closer to volleyball in form, with the ball being passed among six or nine team members. When the ball is hit to a team's side of the net in volleyball, rather than one individual thinking about how to stop or return it, the ball is passed among the team members and then returned to the other side. Of course, there is no rule in conversation that the ball must be returned within three hits as in volleyball, but the conversational ball is moved among teammates and then expelled outside. That is, a topic of conversation is started, give-and-take is carried out concerning it, and it then goes out from one's midst. Then the same process occurs for another topic. In this way, it is appropriate to compare Japanese conversation to the movement of the ball among the members of a volleyball team, in contrast to the give-and-take between two clearly-defined sides in tennis.

In this way, if you should ask a person in a group for directions in Japan, that person will not answer you directly even if he or she should know the answer. Rather, that Japanese person will first consult with the others, asking about the way or confirming it, and then answer you only after getting their answers. Sometimes you will not even be answered by the person you asked but by someone with some special qualifications that has been consulted.

The topic is thus passed around like a volleyball. Volleyball is a team game and returning the ball is a joint matter involving all members of the group. One cannot refuse to hit a ball because a teammate's pass was bad; one must try to return even a poorly hit ball, and, on the other hand, when hitting a ball to one's teammate, one must hit it in a way that he or she will be able to respond to it easily. And this pattern is remarkably similar to the principles of conversation in Japanese.

Ringo-o itsutsu-hodo kudasai

Another aspect of Japanese conversation can be seen in the use of the group of words made up of *gurai* (about, . . . or so), *bakari* (about, around; only), *hodo* (about; as . . . as) and the like. These are usually used modifying another word, as in *itsutsu-gurai, itsutsu-bakari,* or *itsutsu-hodo* (about five of them).

If we look up *gurai* in a Japanese dictionary, the definition will go something like this: "Expresses an approximate degree or extent; expresses limits or bounds. Example, *Jippon-gurai aru* (There are about ten of them)." Certainly all of these words express degree, as in the sentences

> *Sanjuu-nin-gurai atsumatta* (About thirty people came).
> *Ichiman-nin-bakari sanka-shita* (About 10,000 persons participated).
> *Kyoo-wa, sanjuu-do-hodo aru* (Today it is up to 30°C/101°F).

However, if we closely examine how these words are used in actual conversation, we will see that they are not always used to express degree. In fact, they are used in a considerably different meaning. At vegetable stands or bakeries and the like in particular, a considerable percentage of the time these words are not used merely to express degree or amount.

In sentences like

> *Niku-o sanbyaku-guramu-hodo kudasai* (Please give me about 300 grams of meat)

and

> *Piinattsu-o nihyaku-guramu-bakari kudasai* (Please give me about 200 grams of peanuts)

we can say that the buyer is indicating that about that weight will do since it is difficult to cut off exactly three-hundred grams of meat. But we also find people using these words for things that are easily countable, such as apples or oranges. Although it is clearly possible to specify five or ten, they will say:

> *Itsutsu-bakari kudasai* (Please give me about five of them)

or

> *Too-hodo kudasai* (Please give me about ten of them).

There are individual differences in this case, also, and not all people use *gurai* or *hodo* in this way. The use of this pattern also seems to vary according to place. In the city of Tokyo, not many people living in apartment complexes (*danchi*) use it, but it is quite common in *shitamachi*, the older, more closely-knit neighborhoods in the city.

One might expect it to be used more often in the provinces, but that is not always the case. When I questioned about two hundred persons in Iwate Prefecture in northern Japan, an overwhelming majority indicated they used *itsutsu-gurai* or *too-hodo*. Young people also used it quite a lot. However, when I asked about this at a lecture in Hikone in Shiga Prefecture in central Japan, out of the approximately two hundred people present, only three or four answered that they use this pattern.

Consideration toward others

It is impossible to indicate the exact cause without

further research, but it is a fact that phrases like *Itsutsu-gurai* or *too-hodo* not indicating an exact amount have a high frequency of use. Of course they will not be used in cases like supermarkets where one can shop without talking to the shopkeeper, but in a bakery, one may very well say something like *"Oishisoona chiizu-keeki-ne. Sono chiizukeeki itsutsu kudasai-na"* (That's good-looking cheesecake. Please give me five pieces of it). In this kind of situation, the pattern *itsutsu-gurai* or *itsutsu-hodo kudasai* is used quite often.

It would indicate a breakdown in communication if, when the buyer said *"Itsutsu-gurai kudasai"* (Give me about five of them), the shopkeeper or clerk then asked, "By 'about five,' do you mean four or six?" In English, we can imagine someone asking "Four or six?" if he is told, "Give me about five." But in Japan it is understood that this phrase means the customer wants five, and the shopkeeper will put that many in a bag without asking.

But what is the function of this *gurai* or *hodo*? Since the number is definite, there is no need to add *hodo* or *gurai*. By doing so, however, the Japanese avoid imposing their will on others through using a clear-cut form of expression. That is, even though the speaker wants exactly five apples or five pieces of cake, he or she will use this pattern indicating an approximate number out of consideration toward the listener. The listener, on the other hand, will interpret this to mean that the speaker really wants five; communication has been successfully effected. The function of *gurai* and *hodo* in this case is thus consideration toward the listener (*omoiyari*). The buyer does not make a unilateral decision or issue an order but seeks a commonality of will, with the listener participating in the decision as well.

Does *hai*＝yes and *iie*＝no?

As mentioned earlier, the exchange of conversation within a group in Japan makes every effort to avoid injuring or denying the other group members. The use of *iie* (no) is another example of that. In the dictionary, *iie* is defined as a word expressing negation, but what exactly does it negate or deny? The Japanese are inclined to simply equate *hai* with "yes" and *iie* with "no," and English-speakers studying Japanese are also taught that and use them that way. However, they later begin to notice that the Japanese actually use them quite differently. Soon they will suggest that the Japanese *hai* and *iie* are not actually equivalent to the English "yes" and "no."

It is clear that *iie* is a negative. In what sort of situations is it used?

lie as a humble word

When I examined the use of *iie* in film scenarios, I found that it was largely used to deny or negate what another person had said — and in the overwhelming majority of cases, it had the additional function of showing the modesty or humility of the speaker. For example,

    A: *Yoku eego-ga odeki-ni narimasu-ne.* (You speak English very well.)

    B: *Iie, totemo watashi-wa . . .* (No, I am very bad at it.)

or

    A: *Okosan-ga, yoku odeki-ni natte.* (Your child does well in school.)

    B: *Iie, uchi-no-wa totemo deki-ga warukute.* (No, our child isn't so smart.)

A similar use is shown in these examples:

    A: *Watashi-wa yappari dame-desu-ne.* (I really am hopeless.)

B: *Iie, anata-wa hontoo-wa chikara-ga aru-n-desu-yo.* (No, you really are an able person.)

and

A: *Totemo naorisoo-mo nai-na.* (It doesn't seem like I'll ever get well.)

B: *Iya, sugu naorimasu-yo.* (No, you'll recover in no time.)

As we can see in these examples, *iie* is often used to humble oneself in disagreeing with the other person or to encourage and comfort someone.

Iie used to oppose others

Iie is used in the same way as the English "no," that is, to state that another is wrong, only in very limited circumstances. One case is the classroom, where one is permitted, even encouraged, to judge the facts of a matter and disagree if necessary, as in this exchange:

Teacher: *Ni tasu ni-wa yon-desu-ne. Sore-dewa, ni tasu san-wa roku-desu-ka.* (Two and two are four, aren't they? Now, are two and three, six?)

Student: *Iie, chigaimasu.* (No, they aren't.)

One can also use *iie* in the case of a simple transmission of information not seriously affecting the interests of the people involved, as in this exchange between a section boss and worker early in the morning:

Section boss: *Yamada-kun-wa, moo kite-iru-kane.* (Has Yamada come yet?)

Worker: *Iie, mada-desu.* (No, not yet.)

The major requirement for this use of *iie* is that the values and judgment of, at the very least, the persons participating in the conversation are not called into question. Conversely, aside from these limited cases, the use of *iie* to oppose others is almost totally restricted to arguments and other disputes. Generally speaking, it is most distressing, and even painful, for the Japanese to respond to an invitation like

    Doo-da, ippai yaran-ka (How about going out for a drink?)

or

    Doo-da, koohii-demo nomi-ni ikanai-ka (Won't you have some coffee with me?)

with *iie*, as in,

    Iie, kekkoo-desu (No, I don't want to)

or

    Iie, kyoo-wa dame-desu (No, I can't do it today).

Individual differences exist, of course, and particularly some young people will easily refuse an invitation with *iie*. In this case, the person to whom this easy, light *iie* has been said may well feel hurt by it. As we have said, however, most Japanese find it extremely difficult and painful to use *iie* when the way of thinking, judgment, or values of the other person are involved, and we might even say that there is a cultural rule in effect in Japan that *iie* not be used in this case.

'Ichioo kangaete-okimashoo'

Of course, the Japanese cannot always act in accordance with the wishes of others. At times they must express opposition, and they have various ways of doing so, one of which is illustrated in the following anecdote.

Once an American student studying Japanese came to me and complained that the Japanese in government offices are always lying. He said that they had made a promise to him last week, but when he went this week they said they never made any such promise. When I asked him what it was about, he said he had gone there about a visa problem. Due to circumstances, he had received his previous visa under less than ideal conditions. Now he had to extend that visa, but they said that he would have to leave the country once and then return. It was inconvenient for him to do this so he had gone to see if the visa couldn't somehow be extended without his leaving the country. At some time during those talks, one of the officials there, probably because he was so persistent, seems to have said, *"Sore-ja, ichido kangaete-okimashoo"* (In that case, let's think it over).

In this case, *ichioo* (once, in outline, tentatively, in general) is not being used as an affirmative. Judged in context, we can conclude that it was used as a signal to close the conversation. However, that American student thought that *ichioo kangaeru* (to think about in principle) indicated a real effort to reconsider the problem and left saying he would come back in a week. Then when he went back there again, the official said that he had never indicated there was a chance of being able to renew his visa without leaving the country, and, moreover, he had not told him to come back again. The student, however, had gone there with the understanding that they probably would have been able to take care of the problem by then.

'I recognize your wishes but cannot comply with them'

Certain expressions in Japanese such as *ichioo*, *tonikaku* (at any rate), *maamaa* (well, probably), and *doryoku-shite-miyoo* (We'll make an effort) often cause problems during international exchanges since they are regarded by foreigners as empty words. The Japanese dislike flatly saying no to others. They therefore use these expressions to recognize the desires and feelings of others when they cannot agree with them. *Ichioo yatte-mimashoo* (We'll try in principle to do it) means that theoretically there might possibly be a chance of doing something, but practically speaking there is no chance at all. Since it is very difficult for the Japanese to come right out and state that something is impossible, they use this communication pattern to convey this message to the other person through the words *ichi-oo* or *doryoku-suru* instead.

Thus, in this case, a considerable gap exists between the linguistic form and the actual meaning of the utterance, and an element of individual difference also must be considered. That is, there is a different degree of possible expectation of results according to the person using these words. A wide range is left to the judgment of the listener — that person used *ichioo* so there's a fair chance, that person said *doryoku-suru* so there's no chance at all, and so on.

To summarize, it is against the rules of the Japanese speech community to deny what others have said; one recognizes the wishes of others and endeavors to follow them as much as possible. Since, however, it is impossible for human beings to totally go along with the expectations and wishes of others, the Japanese have had to somehow find a point of compromise on what is actually possible and devise expressions to convey that compromise.

AN ORIENTATION TOWARD
SHARED EXPERIENCE AND KNOWLEDGE (1)

'Please don't forget anything when you get off'

The strong Japanese orientation toward shared feelings, judgments, and desires tends to lead to slighting any search for the rights and wrongs, the pluses and minuses, of a matter. The possibility also exists that any concern with whether or not one's thoughts and desires have been communicated, with whether or not the facts of the matter have been conveyed, will be weakened. Consideration toward the other (*omoiyari*) will lead the listener as well to give something less than a clear and direct response to an utterance; an excess of *omoiyari* is often displayed by the Japanese even when one appeals to them to answer frankly and directly.

Along with *hai*, the expression *Soo-desu-ne* (That's right; You have a point there) is often cited by foreigners as a problematic response in Japanese. They will give some opinion, such as "Japan should take more responsibility in regard to the world economy." A Japanese will reply, *"Soo-desu-ne."* The foreigner therefore thinks that Japanese has agreed with his or her opinion, but then later the same Japanese will say something in direct opposition to that, as "However, Japan's economic power is in reality very weak, and it is very difficult for her to take responsibility toward the other countries of the world."

In the operation of *omoiyari*, as seen in the vague use of *Soo-desu-ne*, a person decides that the other person is acting out of a certain way of thinking and that, accordingly, it would be kind to the other to respond in a certain way. If this *omoiyari* is carried too far, however, it becomes *osekkai*, officious kindness or meddling. For example, consider the announcements in the buses, trains, and subways in Japan.

These announcements do not stop at announcing when the train will leave or what the next station is, but go on to tell the passengers to please not forget anything when they get off, to be careful when getting off, to not forget their umbrellas, and so forth. Foreigners find the announcement not to forget anything especially annoying. They feel that whether one forgets anything or not is one's own responsibility, and it is strange to have this announced in the trains and buses. When this matter is called to their attention, the Japanese may agree that these announcements can be annoying at times, but they do not feel that the station employees are interfering or doing anything particularly bad.

'Now be careful of cars'

This attitude of Americans and other foreigners arises from their different upbringing; they are also critical of the, to them, overprotective way Japanese mothers talk to their children. Japanese mothers give various warnings and directions to their children even when they have become quite big — "do this," "do that," "don't do that," or, when the children are going out, "be careful of cars," and "be sure to come home early." These latter warnings have become standard patterns used by mothers seeing off their children. And this is not limited to children; they treat their husbands in the same way. These admonitions given to children of junior high or high school age when they are leaving for school are difficult for many foreigners to understand. Of course, American mothers will also warn their children to watch out for cars when they go out, but this is limited to times when there is some special reason for doing so, such as a recent traffic accident. They will warn them to take special care, but not everyday day in and day out for five or even ten years as in Japan. Such foreigners feel that this Japanese pattern is a very annoying one which treats children as younger than their age and treats adults like children.

If one thinks about it, the announcements in the trains not to forget anything and the like are intrusive. The Japanese, however, regard them as consideration toward others (*omoiyari*), as something which should be said. When traveling abroad, the Japanese often find the scarcity of announcements in the various public transportation systems inconvenient, regardless of the question of whether or not one is reminded not to forget anything. In fact, at one time there was talk in Japan about whether it wasn't inconsiderate to foreign travelers not to have special English announcements on the bullet trains when there was some mechanical difficulty stopping the train along with the regular English announcements about where the train was stopping and so forth.

Often the announcements in the subway and trains cannot be heard clearly, and sometimes even the Japanese cannot understand what is being said. One may doubt whether a communication which fails to be conveyed to the listener can really be called *omoiyari*; perhaps we should rather view that as a reflection of the low value placed on the spoken language in Japan.

'How much is this?' — 'That's very cheap'

One can also find examples of *osekkai*, officious kindness, in stores. One foreign student told me he disliked going to department stores and other stores in Japan because he could never get a direct answer to his questions.

We have already briefly discussed one investigation of Japanese language behavior relevant to his problem: the investigation by Ouchi Shigeo concerning what responses were given to the question "How much is this?"

We would expect such replies as "It's 3000 yen" or "That's 5000 yen," but this research predicted that the actual responses would be somewhat different and in fact they soon ran across answers like "Which one?" (*Dore-desu-ka*) or "Oh, that one?" (*A, sore-desu-ka*). A typical exchange would be as follows:

    Buyer: *Kore ikura-desu-ka.* (How much is this?)
    Clerk: *Dore-desu-ka.* (Which one?)
    Buyer: *Kore-desu.* (This one.)
    Clerk: *A, sore-wa, sanzen-en-desu.* (Oh, that's 3000 yen.)

This question, "Which one?", is a relative one born out of the language situation itself and of course will appear in English and other languages as well as Japanese.

But a more significant form of response was also found. At times the shopkeepers would respond to "How much is this?" with "Oh, that's very cheap now" or "Oh, that's a good value for the price." To a child they might say, "That's not something for children" (*Sore-wa, kodomo-no mono-ja nai-yo*).

On reflection, Japanese will realize they often receive indirect responses to their direct questions about the price or nature of an article, such as "That's a good value" or "That's just right for you." Moreover, these indirect responses generally concern the situation, values, and interests of the buyer. This too can thus be thought of as a form of *omoiyari*, or consideration toward the listener.

'Are motte-kite-kure'

This consideration toward others implies certain expectations toward others. Trying to understand the standpoint and thinking of others, conversely, means one expects others to understand one's own standpoint and feelings. As touched upon in Chapter 2, the words *kore* (this one), *sore* (that one), and *are* (that one over there) have an extremely high frequency of use in Japanese, and *are* in particular carries with it the expectation that the listener will understand what is being referred to indirectly in this way.

Typical of the sort of sentence with *are* often appearing in everyday conversation is, "*Are, motte-kite-kure*" (Please bring that) or "*Are, doo natte-iru-kana*" (What's happening with that?). These are used both at home and at work by, in the majority of cases, those of higher ranking in the group — the older person (*senpai*), the head of the household, or the father.

At home, most requests in the form *"Are motte-kite-kure"* (Please bring that), *"Motte-kite-kure"* (Please bring it), or even just *"Are"* (That) will mean something like *"Tabako-o motte-koi"* (Bring my cigarettes) or *"Koohii-ga nomitai-n-da"* (I want some coffee). At work, one will use *"Are, doo natta"* (How did that turn out?) to mean something like "How's the drawing up of papers concerning the contract problem with A company that we discussed yesterday coming along?" or "What were the results of the telephone call that I asked you to make to B company yesterday?"

Obviously enough, these sentences could have been expressed in full as *"Tabako-o motte-kite-kure"* (Please bring my cigarettes) and *"Koohii-ga nomitai"* (I want some coffee), or *"A-sha-e okuru shorui-wa tsukutta-ka"* (Have you drawn up the papers to send to A company?) and *"B-sha-to-no renraku-wa doo natta-ka"* (What was the result of the contact with B company?), and in that form anyone would be able to understand them. The speaker, however, has chosen to use *are* instead, a form of communication assuming the listener will sufficiently grasp the meaning from just this limited hint. Thus the word *are* presupposes the existence of common experience, knowledge, and information on the part of the speaker and listener; a listener without that background will have no clue to the meaning when another says *"Are doo shita"* (What happened about that?) or *"Are, tanomu"* (Please take care of that).

English seems to lack any real equivalent to the use of this *are*. Although "it" is sometimes used in a similar way, it is not comparable to *are* in broadness or frequency of use. Nor does English have a set of words equivalent to the *kore, sore, are,* and *dore* (which one?) words discussed in Chapter 2. Accordingly, the proper use of *are* and *sore* is very difficult for foreigners. Even foreigners who have been speaking Japanese for five or ten years and are quite fluent in it frequently make mistakes with them, particularly with the use premised on the existence of experience or information held in common by the speaker and the listener. Almost all foreigners will mix up *are* and *sore* when asked to fill in the blanks in the following test passage:

—*Rashoomon-to yuu eega, mita-kai. Are-wa ii eega-da-na.* (Have you seen *Rashomon*? It's a good movie.)

—*Sore-wa doo yuu eega-da.* (What kind of movie is it?)

One can use *are* if, as in the first sentence, one has some knowledge about that movie or has seen it, but if one is unfamiliar with that movie, as in the second sentence, one must choose *sore*.

Similarly, when someone says, *"Kinoo-wa, Takaoka-e itte-kita-n-da-yo"* (I went to Takaoka yesterday), a foreigner is apt to say, *"Asoko-wa, donna tokoro-deshita-ka"* (What was it like?). But *asoko* (over there) is used only for places one has been to or about which one has considerable knowledge; in this case, *soko* should be used.

Since *are* presupposes the existence of common experience or knowledge between the speaker and listener, students will realize they should know what a lecturer is referring to by *are* and will search their minds for that mutual knowledge when the lecturer says something like *"Are-wa nannen-gurai mae-no koto-deshita-ka-ne"* (Now how many years ago was that I wonder) or *"Are-wa doo natte-iru-n-deshoo-ka"* (I wonder how that has turned out).

Nani (what) and *rei-no* (usual, customary; also used to refer to something often talked about) are also used in the same way as *are*, as in these sentences:

Nani-wa ima doo shite-iru-kana. (I wonder how that person is doing now.)

and
> *Rei-no doo natta-kana.* (I wonder how that turned out.)

Senjitsu-wa doomo . . .

The above patterns are used in certain limited situations, but greetings also display the same inclination toward stressing shared experience. One typical form is the customary reference to their last meeting when two Japanese meet. For example, these set phrases are often heard—
> *Senjitsu-wa taihen gochisoosama-deshita.* (literally, I received a great feast the other day.)

and
> *Sono setsu-wa taihen goyakkai-ni narimashita.* (literally, I received much care from you on that occasion.)

Americans will ask how many times they should continue to say *"Senjitsu-wa gochisoosama"*; this use seems strange to them since in English they do not usually talk about a party or dinner the next time they meet. But for the Japanese, such expressions confirm the existence of a shared experience, thereby strengthening their solidarity and sense of unity.

A dislike of change

We can draw one conclusion from this kind of language use: for the Japanese, the existing status quo, including human relationships, is desirable and change is to be avoided. Europeans and Americans, on the other hand, presuppose change and think it impossible to have a state of affairs continue unchanged. Certainly the Japanese show a conservative side in their formation of set systems while doing some job. Of course this is a question of degree, and it is rash to lump together Europe and the United States and to speak of them as one entity, but at the very least we can say that if one were to presume to make that sort of cultural comparison, one key element would have to be this attitude to change, whether one anticipates and hopes for change or not. As a general rule, the Japanese dislike change and partings. On the other hand, Americans think of partings as inevitable, even among friends.

In a certain sense, the different attitudes toward change over time are related to differing expectations toward others. That is, the two opposing standpoints exist of expecting and not expecting people to vary from person to person.

In this way, strong pressures are present at meetings in Japan for all to come to the same opinion. If even one person is opposed, it is very difficult to resolve this conflict and majority opinions somehow leave a bad aftertaste. Most foreigners, on the other hand, feel it is inevitable that there will be those with differing opinions, and it is all present having the same opinion that is unthinkable. And, as we have seen in this chapter and the previous one, this Japanese view that there is a problem if all are not in agreement is clearly reflected in the patterns of spoken Japanese.

AN ORIENTATION TOWARD
SHARED EXPERIENCE AND KNOWLEDGE (2)
— The tendency to take a relative standpoint —

No standard second-person pronoun

In pointing out tendencies in Japanese toward harmony and unity and toward shared experience and knowledge, we are not saying that these form an exclusive norm that the Japanese follow all the time. Alongside the tendency toward the joint or shared clearly exists one toward the independent and the individual, and we cannot overlook the strong consciousness of hierarchial relationships and status. Harmony and unity are limited to the united group and will first come into play when an insider consciousness is formed.

While we must keep these limitations in mind, we can also see the tendency toward shared experience and knowledge in interpersonal behavior in Japan, in how the individual is treated. One such area is how people are referred to and how personal pronouns are used. No standard second-person pronoun exists in Japanese, so that one is never sure how to address another person. English is much more convenient in this respect since one can just use "you" in all situations, without having to choose the correct form of address from among the many possible words indicating different levels of politeness, respect, and familiarity such as *kimi*, *anata*, and *omae*.

One's mother-in-law is also *okaasan*

In other respects, however, Japanese is more convenient than English. For example, the Japanese directly address both their mothers and mothers-in-law as *okaasan* (Mother) and their fathers and fathers-in-law as *otoosan* (Father). In English, one calls one's own mother "Mother" or "Mom" or the like, but not one's mother-in-law. Thus, young American couples are often troubled about how to address their spouse's parents. Calling them by their last name, as in "Mr. Johnson," sounds too formal, but, on the other hand, it does not seem right somehow to call them by their first name. Each family finds its own solution to this problem. Sometimes the mother will suggest what she would like to be called, perhaps asking her daughter-in-law to call her by her first name. An American wife may thus call her mother-in-law Catherine, but it is hard to imagine even the most modern or internationalized Japanese wife calling her mother-in-law Hanako or Akiko or the like.

This extended use of *okaasan* or *otoosan* is not limited to one's parents-in-law, but is also employed toward the parents of one's friends, as when one is visiting a friend's house. One interpretation of this pattern is that husbands and wives address their parents-in-law from the viewpoint of the spouse and that, similarly, friends address a friend's parents from the standpoint of that friend.

'*Boku, ikutsu?*'

In the same way, adults will address young boys as *boku*, the word used by men and boys for "I." A man or woman might say to a child playing in the park, "*Boku, nani yatte asonde-iru-no*" (What are you playing at?; literally, What am I playing at?). This use is difficult for foreign students of Japanese to understand, but in this case also, the speaker is taking the standpoint of the listener.

Although this can be a convenient and effective means of communication, it is open to ambiguity. For example, consider the following sentence: "*Boku-ga nani-o shita-ka, chanto otoosan-ni iinasai-yo*" (Tell [your] father what [you] have done). In this case, who is *boku*, who is *otoosan*, and who is saying "tell him"? *Boku* might be a child and *otoosan* might be the speaker. Or the speaker might be the mother of a boy telling him to do that. Another possibility is that the speaker is an adult telling someone else's child to tell his father what he has done.

Many other examples like this one could be given. They do not cause problems in actual communication, however, because of the context; in context it will be clear who *boku*, *otoosan*, and the speaker are.

Now what was grandmother's first name?

However, this way of referring to people seems to influence how one looks at other people. One interesting phenomenon is that many Japanese cannot clearly remember the first names of their grandparents. Of the people I asked, most could give the name of their grandfather readily enough, but few could give the name of their grandmother, even though they all had clear memories of playing with her or receiving graduation gifts from her. This is true for aunts and uncles, great-aunts and great-uncles, as well. The Japanese usually call them simply *ojisan* (uncle) or *obasan* (aunt) so even if they have visited them often, they find it difficult to remember their name when writing them a letter.

We may interpret this phenomenon as evidence that the Japanese customarily regard other persons not as individuals, i.e. in terms of their own individuality and name, but in terms of their relationship to them. Consequently, when it is necesssary to distinguish among one's aunts and uncles, one does so not by name, as in Yamada Taro or Suzuki Ichiro, but by some other means such as place, as in *inaka-no ojisan* (the uncle in the country) or *Koojimachi-no obasan* (the aunt in Kojimachi). The same method is used for one's parents and parents-in-law.

In direct address, one's spouse's parents are called *okaasan* and *otoosan*, but when it is necessary to specify in conversation which spouse's parents are meant, one says something like *Kanda-no okaasan* (the mother in Kanda) or *Ikebukuro-no otoosan-no ie-ni itte-kita* (I went to the Ikebukuro father's house). If one were to use a name, it would be the last name, as in *Itoo-no ie-e* (to Ito's house), and not the first name.

Stressing what a person or thing belongs to

This characteristic way of referring to others is in

line with something often pointed out in discussions of Japanese culture — the Japanese identify themselves in terms of the company they work for rather than occupation. A Japanese will tend to say he works for such and such company before saying he is an engineer or the like, but even more significant is the relative weakness of the desire to convey one's personal name to the listener in Japan.

Other evidence shows that the Japanese consider other persons not in terms of individual character and personality, but rather in terms of status, job, relationships, and the like. Take, for example, the expression *mibun-shoomeisho* (literally, proof of status). In English, this is called an identification or ID card. The use of the words "identity" in English and *mibun*, or "status," in Japanese clearly reveals the different ways of thinking about people in the two cultures.

We can say that to what one belongs constitutes an important standard in regarding not only people, but also in thinking about things. When thinking about the relations between human beings and other things, the Japanese are concerned with who owns a thing or what interest people have in it, rather than with the thing itself. And the Japanese language clearly distinguishes between people and things. For example, *sumu* (to reside) and *kurasu* (to live) are used only for human beings, *ikiru* (to live, to be alive) is used mainly for human beings and animals, and *kareru* (to wither) is used only for plants. In other words, the Japanese distinguish animate beings and inanimate objects from human beings, and tend to describe them not in terms of themselves but of their relations with human beings; this matter will be discussed further later in this book.

Chapter 5. The Special Characteristics of Spoken Japanese (3)
— The concern with relative relationships —

THE CONCERN WITH RELATIVE ADVANTAGE AND DISADVANTAGE (1)
— Toward other people —

'Deploring inequality'
　During the period of Japan's high economic growth, the phrase *mooretsu-shain*, or zealous company man, was popular, and those who gave themselves body and soul to work were well-regarded. But with the coming to an end of this high economic growth and the increasing talk of bad economic times, those who can maintain good relations with others and are skilled in teamwork are sought instead of the *mooretsu-shain*. Perhaps the time is right once again for the ancient phrase "deploring not poverty, but inequality" (*mazushiki-o ureezu, hitoshikarazaru-o ureu*).
　This "deploring of inequality" can be sighted in various areas of Japanese life. If we look just at dress, considerable variety has been present in recent years, and such catch phrases as "respect for individuality" (*kosei-no sonchoo*) and "giving rein to individuality" (*kosei-o ikasu*) have appeared. But in spite of that, the members of any given social group in Japan all tend to wear the same outfit, as in the dark blue or black suits of the organization men; and school or work uniforms are also popular. Or take disco dancing, the very essence of free, individualized movement. In Japan, even disco dancing becomes highly stylized with one particular way of dancing deemed *the* way to do it.

Similarly, as soon as jeans and an informal look became socially acceptable, all went out and started wearing the same kind of jeans. Perhaps we can regard this, too, as an example of the philosophy of deploring inequality. Certainly the Japanese dislike the creation of any disparity among persons.

A dislike of evaluation

At one time, efficiency ratings were a cause of controversy in Japan. Americans often wanted to know why one could not make efficiency ratings of employees in Japan, and did not seem altogether convinced by the explanations offered by the Japanese.

The Japanese have an abhorrence of openly conducted evaluations. Efficiency rating systems are now widespread but are not generally conducted openly. Some are done secretly, and some are so formalized that they have lost all meaning as an evaluation.

Another common example of an evaluation of others is the letter of recommendation. When a Japanese professor has written a letter of recommendation, however, Americans do not place much faith in it. Most Japanese letters of recommendation simply recommend without any real attempt at evaluation; they praise all, not just the truly superior, and avoid any explicit statement of strong and weak points.

In the United States, however, the letter of recommendation is not a purely formal mechanism, but serves a real purpose, and the Americans think that it should make a just evaluation of the person being recommended. Thus they will write differently about different university or graduate students. Similarly, although it is difficult for the Japanese with their lifetime employment system to imagine, a letter of recommendation from one's superior at the former job is necessary when a worker changes jobs, and that letter is one important factor in setting the new salary.

It may be going too far to say that Americans positively like evaluations, but making evaluations is a well-established American custom. This acceptance of evaluation can also be seen in the common practice of university students evaluating their teachers. Students will often collect and put out a book of several hundred pages of student evaluations of each professor; these evaluations are quite explicit and severe — for example, Professor X is poor at the presentation of problems or Professor Y's explanations are unclear. (Of course, the university makes its own separate evaluations of the professors.) This would be unthinkable in Japan, and even at the peak of the student movement and campus disturbances, I recall no publication of ratings of professors even though there were incidents where professors were threatened with violence.

'I'm poor at languages so please teach me accordingly'

American students not only evaluate their professors, but think it natural that they themselves be evaluated in their classes. The frequency of testing is higher than in Japan, and American students expect regular quizzes in language classes. Of course, they do not actually like quizzes, but they may well criticize a teacher who does not give them. Some time ago, one foreign student came to me at the end of a year's study of Japanese. In the most basic class, he was a conscientious student who had studied hard all year. He complained to me that even though he was not very good at languages, I had not adjusted my teaching accordingly.

One cannot imagine a Japanese student complaining to his teacher in this way since the Japanese are as frightened of being different from others in the classroom as elsewhere. Outside the classroom, this fear leads the Japanese to buy the same things as the people next door and to socialize as much as other people in the neighborhood. More passively, it takes the form of trying not to deviate from others in any way. The Japanese are also very sensitive toward language behavior that makes distinctions between people. In everyday spoken Japanese, distinctions based on social position and status certainly exist, but the Japanese, especially in the mass media, are very receptive to criticism of that as a bad thing. This would seem to reflect their true feelings.

'Kaite-moratte-yatte-kudasai'

Wanting to be the same as others and deploring all not being equal, is not necessarily the same as being unconcerned with whether one is better or worse off than others. On the contrary, the Japanese are very sensitive to being worse off than others. It is just that evaluating others is very painful for the Japanese, and they prefer to meet face to face and have give-and-take about their mutual interests, confirming these interests and searching for some compromise. Accordingly, the Japanese language is very rich in expressions used to negotiate with others.

The following sentence is a typical one expressing the relative relations of the speaker and listener and their relative advantage and disadvantage: *"Kaite-moratte-yatte-kudasaimasen-ka"* (Won't you have it written for us?). This sentence cannot be fully translated into English; it is not enough to indicate that someone has asked someone to do something. In *moratte-yatte* (you are kind enough to receive the favor) and *kudasaimasen-ka* (won't you do me the favor?), the giving and receiving relations are explicitly expressed. The phrase *kaite-moratte-yatte* (receive the favor of having it written) indicates that the writer is not the listener but a third person, that the listener will be the recipient of the third person writing it, and that the listener will thereby benefit the third person and the speaker. One would have to make a lengthy explanation to express all of that in English. In other words, the words *morau* (receive), *yaru* (give), and *kudasaru* (give) used here do not simply indicate the action of giving or receiving but also who benefits by that action; other words used in this way include *itadaku* (receive), *ageru* (give), *sashiageru* (give), and *kureru* (give).

Interestingly enough, Japanese is at the same time weak in clearly expressing such human relations as, in the above sentence, who the writer is, who is going to receive the written material, and who is asking for it. In English, one method used to express these relations is the active and passive voice. For example, corresponding to the active sentence "He opened the window" is the passive sentence "The window was opened." The Japanese are taught this pattern in English class from junior high school, but it cannot be transferred directly into Japanese; Japanese has no passive corresponding exactly to this English passive.

'Enpitsu-ga kezurareta-yo'

One can, of course, say "He opened the window" in Japanese: *Mado-o aketa*. But can one say *Mado-wa akerareta* or *Mado-ga akeraremashita-yo* for "The window was opened"? One can say *Enpitsu-o kezuru* for "I sharpen the pencil," but what about *Enpitsu-ga kezurareta-yo* for "The pencil is sharpened"? Although the Japanese will write those kinds of Japanese sentences as translations of English sentences, they are not natural Japanese sentences. Some may argue that even though *Enpitsu-ga kezurareta* is strange, there are expressions in Japanese using the passive such as *Tatakai-*

no hibuta-wa kirareta (Fighting commenced), but this type of expression occurs only in abstract and literary written sentences. No, this passive construction cannot usually be found in spoken Japanese.

'Nakarete komatta'

The Japanese learn in junior high school grammar classes that *-reru* and *-rareru* are verb endings indicating respect and potentiality as well as the passive. However, as stated above, this passive is not an expression reversing the doer and receiver of an action, as in English; words with *-reru* and *-rareru* in Japanese express the evaluations and emotional attitude of the speaker. For example, above I said that the sentence *Enpitsu-ga kezurareta* does not exist, but actually it is possible to say this in certain situations, as in *Enpitsu-o kezurarete, komatchatteru-n-da* (I'm inconvenienced because someone sharpened the pencil).

In this case, *-rareru* is used in a situation where someone other than the speaker has sharpened the speaker's pencil and thereby inconvenienced him because he wanted it left unsharpened. This pattern can be used in Japanese not only for transitive verbs where someone is performing some action on an object, but also with intransitive verbs such as cry (*naku*) or laugh (*warau*), as in *nakarete komatta* (I was troubled by his/her crying) or *warawarete oojoo-shita* (Their laughing put me in an awkward position). Clearly this form of expression, often referred to as the suffering passive, differs considerably from the passive in English. In essence, the speaker is trying to determine his or her advantage in relation to others. The Japanese language is very sensitive to the relative advantage of the speaker and listener — or perhaps we should say that the users of Japanese are very sensitive to the relative advantage of the speaker and listener.

The on-the-spot evaluation done with the other

These -*reru* and -*rareru* forms, as well as such verbs as *yaru* (give) and *morau* (receive), are used very frequently in everyday life — thereby expressing the speaker's satisfaction or dissatisfaction and judgment of relative advantage and disadvantage. Any society possesses norms and rules larger than the individual listener and speaker, but these norms and rules are not in operation in this situation. Rather we can see here the common Japanese tendency for the speaker and the listener to meet, talk, reach some compromise, and assent to who is losing and gaining in a particular situation. In other words, conversation is not conducted according to societal norms, but rather standards are decided each time in the context of the relative relations of the speaker and listener. This proceeding by a mutual evaluation of advantage and disadvantage can also be seen in the practice of Japanese businessmen abroad of arranging transactions by conferring with others in person rather than by telephone or letter.

We must, of course, recognize considerable individual variation in the actual use of words such as *yaru* and *morau* and of those ending in -*reru* and -*rareru* — ones we have given as evidence of the Japanese sensitivity to relative advantage and disadvantage. Some people strongly dislike these expressions and will avoid them, while others will use them every time they open their mouths. We will touch upon these individual differences later, but at the very least, friction is highly probable in communications between individuals who have different philosophies regarding this concern with relative advantage and disadvantage. Another important consideration is the possible interference of this language pattern in foreign-language study.

THE CONCERN WITH RELATIVE ADVANTAGE AND DISADVANTAGE (2)
— Toward inanimate objects —

Spotless polished cars

A concern with relative advantage and disadvantage is by no means restricted to the Japanese. Undoubtedly all peoples feel such concern, and, indeed, its lack would be remarkable. The problem, rather, is what form that concern takes. One special characteristic of the Japanese concern toward relative advantage and disadvantage is that it is not limited to human beings alone but also extends toward inanimate objects.

The Japanese have the reputation of cherishing their cars and throwing themselves into cleaning and polishing them, yelling at children who touch them. Westerners, on the other hand, are not usually all that concerned with keeping their cars spotless and seem rather to view the automobile as little more than a tool. Although even a slight touching of the bumpers is treated as a collision in Japan, in the West, the bumper is regarded as a tool to be used, for example, to force one's way into a tight parking space. Similar examples are often given to illustrate how the Japanese differ from Westerners in valuing and taking meticulous care of objects.

Certainly the Japanese do in general carefully maintain and preserve objects. The question, however, is whose objects and what kind of objects. Private cars are carefully cleaned and polished but what about publicly owned cars? The fact is that individuals cherish their own property, but little concern is given to dirty or damaged public facilities.

'*Karita sutoobu-ga koraremashita*'
There is an incident in my personal experience that

illustrates nicely the relationship between inanimate objects and human beings. Some ten years or so ago an American doctoral student in cultural anthropology from Harvard University came to Japan to study Japanese society. She went to live with a farm family in Nagano Prefecture in order to study the human relationships in a Japanese farm village. Since she had been a Japanese-language student of mine, I often saw her when she was in Tokyo. One day she suddenly told me that she had had a fight with her landlord two days before and now he would not talk with her, but she did not understand what the problem was.

She had gone to her landlord two days before to return an oil heater he had lent her several weeks earlier. The moment she handed it to him saying it had broken, he had been out of sorts and would not talk with her. When I asked what words she had used, she could not remember exactly but thought she had said something like, *"Kono-mae-kara karite-ita sutoobu-ga kowarete-shimaimashita"* (The heater that I borrowed from you has broken).

Then I asked about the character and customary way of talking of her landlord. He seemed to be a kind man but something of a busybody who was fussy about small details and was always contriving to start conversations and ask questions. Next I asked her what was wrong with the heater. She was not sure but said it would not light that morning so she had told her landlord that it was broken. Then I explained to her the difference between *kowaremashita* (It broke) and *kowashimashita* (I broke it).

Grammatically speaking, *kowaremashita* is simply the intransitive form of the verb and *kowashimashita* the transitive. In terms of the literal meaning, *kowashimashita* is limited to cases where one bears some direct responsibility in an object's breaking or has deliberately broken it, and *kowaremashita* neutrally expresses the situation of the object breaking by itself. Accordingly, there is nothing to stop one from using *kowaremashita* when something has broken and one feels no particular responsibility in its breaking. However, in actual conversation, the choice of transitive or intransitive indicates one's attitude to the other person and to the object.

Thus, aside from individual and generational differences, those Japanese who speak in an adult, characteristically Japanese way will probably choose *kowashimashita* (I broke it) even when the cause of its breaking is unclear, and it is uncertain whether one bears any responsibility in that or not. In this case, since the heater belonged to the other person and one has borrowed it, one should at least express one's feeling of responsibility for its being broken. Indeed, most Japanese will choose *kowashimashita* to show their sense of responsibility even if the article in question has broken solely because it was of poor quality.

'Iya, anata-no see-dewa arimasen'

But the matter would not end there. The person who lent the article, such as a heater, will then lay the blame on his own property and say something like, "No, it's not your fault. This heater was subject to breakdown from the start. It was more than time for it to break." Then the borrower will again take the blame saying, "No, I am at fault," and the lender will again deny that saying, "No, I am to blame . . ." This pattern of utterances is a fundamental one in Japan for dealing with conflicting interests in words. But that American graduate student could not understand why she should say "I broke it," when she had not done so deliberately.

'I'm sorry'

Of course the above pattern will not be used to debate the responsibility for damage to one's property with someone outside one's circle with whom one has hostile relations. This thought-pattern also causes complications for the Japanese abroad.

It is often pointed out that Japanese abroad overuse the expression "I'm sorry," and behind this tendency lies the custom of starting a discussion of a problem by expressing one's responsibility, as seen in the section above concerning *kowashimashita*. It is not enough, however, to simply advise the Japanese not to use "I'm sorry" when they go abroad. Of course it is not necessary to apologize when something has been broken by accident, but it is another matter entirely if one is clearly to blame for its breaking and yet does not apologize. Such irresponsible behavior will not be well received in momentary contacts with strangers, still less in continuing social relations. The proper use of "I'm sorry" in accordance with the facts of the matter is, rather, the mark of a responsible and adult member of society.

I have been using the word *sekinin* in the above discussion, but I would like to point out here in passing that the Japanese use this word in a way not entirely equivalent to "responsibility," its usual translation in English.

'Taihen tsumaranai mono-desu-ga'

The Japanese custom of speaking slightingly of their own things and highly of other's things is well known. When giving something to another, they say something like, *"Kore-wa taihen tsumaranai mono-desu-ga"* (This is a very trifling thing but . . .) and when entertaining someone, say *"Nani-mo gozaimasen-ga"* (We have nothing to offer you but . . .). The recipient will then respond with something like, *"Konna-ni rippana mono-o. . ."* ([I couldn't accept] such a grand gift) or *"Subarashii gochisoo-desu-ne"* (It's a marvelous meal). Lowering oneself and elevating the other is thus a fundamental pattern in the use of honorifics in Japanese, and we can note its resemblance to the pattern described above of claiming that one is responsible for something and denying the responsibility of the other.

Lowering oneself of course also applies to one's family. The Japanese often say things like "My children have poor grades" or "My children are poor at sports." In response, the listener will say something like "Your children do very well," or search for some other good point to praise. This at times leads to quite exaggerated statements, and not a few children feel unhappy with their parents for always praising other children and disparaging them. As the children get bigger, however, they gradually realize that this way of talking is like an exchange of greetings, is one set pattern of conversation. On the other hand, misunderstandings might very well result if one were to make the same sorts of remarks among Americans.

In Japan, too, recent years have witnessed an increase in the number of people who feel able to freely praise things belonging to themselves or those close to them, and regard this as more honest. Many Japanese now find it difficult to know whether it is better to praise one's family and possessions, or, as in the earlier way, it is correct to speak slightingly of them.

This characteristic Japanese behavior is not limited to cases involving inanimate objects alone. For example, the consciousness of whether one might not be bothering others leads the Japanese to give a reason other than the real one when they unexpectedly drop in on someone. They will usually say something like, *"Sono hen-made kimashita-node, tsuide-ni yorasete-moraimashita"* (We were in the neighborhood so decided to visit you on our way home). On the surface this might be thought of as an apology for not having come especially to see them, but in actuality one says that because it would be more of an imposition on the other if one notified them in advance that one was coming, as they would then have to make special preparations. By saying that, the other does not have to worry about whether or not they have provided a generous enough reception for a guest. The Japanese will therefore use this formula even if they are bringing gifts or have otherwise obviously planned their visit.

At any rate, we can say that the use of patterns lowering oneself and building up others, as in this sort of humble language or in taking the responsibility for something onto oneself, has its foundations in worrying if one might not be a nuisance to others. From a different angle, building up the other would seem to be grounded in the expectation of being built up oneself.

At the same time, there is a Japanese proverb that says that the nail that sticks up will get pounded down. Deep in the hearts of the Japanese is the feeling that they must not deviate much from others. That is the dynamic behind the societal rule that anything that sticks up will be knocked down, and conversely, from the standpoint of the individual, that is the source of one's trying not to stand out from others. Trying to be average and to act the same as others may seem to be a negative process, but at the same time, since all advance in the same way, it can be a strong source of internal unity and of motive energy in pushing the group forward.

INTERACTING WITH OTHERS IN TERMS OF HIGHER-LOWER RELATIONS

Okaki-ni naru **and** *okaki-suru*

The Japanese show a strong consciousness of their

relative relationship to the listener, and honorific forms are based on whether the listener is above or below one in position or social status.

Honorific forms (*keigo*) are divided into the two categories of respect forms (*sonkeigo*) and humble forms (*kenjoogo*). Some examples of respect forms are *irassharu* (to be, go, come), *nasaru* (to do), and *ossharu* (to say); these are used to refer to actions of superiors in place of the neutral forms *iru* (to be), *iku* (to go), *kuru* (to come), *suru* (to do), and *yuu* (to say). Other respect forms follow the pattern *okaki-ni naru* for *kaku* (to write) or *goran-ni naru* for *miru* (to see). On the other hand, one uses humble forms when talking about one's own actions to someone higher. Examples of these forms are *mairu* (be, go, come), *ukagau* (ask, go, come), *moosu* (say), *okaki-suru* (write), and *haiken-suru* (see) for *iru* (be), *iku* (go), *kuru* (come), *kiku* (ask), *yuu* (say), *kaku* (write), and *miru* (see).

Japanese society is very strict about these respect and humble forms, and those who cannot use them correctly are the target of considerable criticism. Those who mix up *okaki-ni naru* and *okaki-suru*, or who know only *goran-ni naru* and not *haiken-suru*, will be judged poor speakers of Japanese.

The honorific forms, both respect and humble, are not the only expressions based on standards of relative status. This higher-lower distinction appears in various areas of Japanese life.

For example, this higher-lower relationship is evident in how people are called. In the case of older and younger brothers, the older one will be called *niisan* ("older brother"), but the younger one will not be called *otooto-san* ("younger brother"). In the same way, an older sister will be called *neesan* ("older sister"), but a younger sister will not be called *imooto-san* ("younger sister"). Of course a third person may say something like *"Otooto-san-wa doo-nasatta"* (What happened to Younger Brother?). However, when one is addressing one's own younger brother, it is impossible to say *otooto-san*, *otooto-chan*, or *"Otooto-san, koko-e irasshai"* (Little Brother, come here). This is true not only within the immediate family but also toward more distant relatives; higher-lower categories are especially marked in the latter case.

The same pattern occurs at work and throughout Japanese society. While it is usual to call one's subordinates Yamada-san or Ito-kun, it is difficult to call a superior, for example one's section chief, Yamada-san. In exceptional cases, the atmosphere of the workplace or the personal relationship with the section chief will permit this, or when an underling is older or close in age to the superior, it is possible. However, in most cases, it is very difficult, if not impossible, to call a section or division chief by name.

The spread of *sensee*

This situation gives rise to the custom of calling people by something other than their proper names. In this way, *sensee*, originally a term of respect for teachers and doctors, has become popular as a convenient way of referring to others respectfully. Even though there are those who assert that *sensee* is not appropriate for those unconnected with education, its range of use has widened, and it is increasingly used toward those who are clearly of higher position and who would be displeased at being called by name. *Sensee* is thus used toward members of the Diet, those in the entertainment world, authors and the like.

The nonprofit Japan Broadcasting Corporation, NHK, has a policy of using *-san* rather than *sensee*, apparently following the guidelines issued by the National Japanese Language Council in *"Kore-kara-no keego* (*keigo*)" (Respect language from now on). However, rather than reversing the tide and encouraging the use of -*san*, this policy has led to criticism of the rudeness of NHK announcers.

'Sensee, sayoonara'

The higher-lower relationship also appears in the use of *sayoonara*; *sayoonara* is used at partings, but it cannot be said to everyone without exception. In elementary school, children are taught to bow to their teacher and say *"Sensee, sayoonara"* (Good-bye, Teacher) in a clear voice, and then to bow and say *"Minasan, sayoonara"* (Good-bye, everyone) to their classmates. Then the teacher bows back to them and says *"Sayoonara."* However, this use of *sayoonara* is exceptional in ordinary Japanese society.

Indeed, I have heard of an elderly professor who was greatly indignant when his college students said *"Jaa, sayoonara"* (Well, good-bye) when leaving at the end of his lecture, and I myself feel less than delighted when students say *sayoonara* to me. Of course, whether the use of *sayoonara* is inappropriate or not also depends on the relationship existing between the teacher and the students, and on the situation. Saying *sayoonara* lightly in a formal atmosphere sounds incongruous, but it may be acceptable at school. And people who use *sayoonara* rather than *shitsuree-shimasu* (I beg your pardon) when parting in a work situation will also be criticized.

Thinking rigidly in terms of superiors and inferiors like this is often deplored in Japan as a remnant of the feudal class system, but the fact remains that many people in present Japanese society will feel that *sayoonara* is rude when used toward superiors.

The rude English used by the Japanese

Adjusting speech according to superior-inferior relations is, of course, not unique to Japan, and in any language polite expressions are used toward those one respects. When the Japanese think that English has no respectful expressions toward superiors, it is a mark of their low level of proficiency in English. For while English does not make use of grammatically set forms like the respect language in Japanese, it is strict in regard to the choice of vocabulary, intonation, and the like. Unfortunately, I often hear it said that the English spoken by Japanese tends to be very rude.

'Your book is very good, Teacher'

Japanese does differ significantly from English in some areas, however. One such area is the attitude toward complimenting or praising others. The Japanese do not regard praise or a compliment as invariably being a good thing, and it is not always safe to praise or compliment someone. Some people will not be pleased if they are complimented on their necktie, for instance.

In particular, the Japanese will not be pleased, and may even be insulted, if something involving their specialty is praised; they have pride in doing their job well and feel that their skill is only natural, not something to be complimented on. For example, what will happen if a student praises a teacher's book, saying, "Your recent book is very well written"?

This statement certainly involves an element of evaluation and that is where the problem lies: evaluating the actions, or the results of the actions, of one's superiors is frowned upon. If one were to say to a doctor, "You give shots very well," it would be dubious if this was really a compliment. It is a matter of some interest that higher-lower relations are involved in this way in the area of praise as well.

The higher-lower criterion

Within respect language (*keego*) lies the category of polite language. The honorific and humble forms express the speaker's respect toward the listener and their relative relationship, but the polite language demonstrates the speaker's politeness. Polite forms include the *-masu* verbal ending, *desu*, and *gozaimasu*. These forms, also, cannot be used in an objective way toward anyone at any time, and the listener may demand a certain level of politeness to be shown toward him or her.

For example, customers will not invariably be pleased with the use of the *-masu* form when they enter a *sushi* shop and the cook asks *"Danna, nan-ni shimasu-ka"* (What will you have, mister?), or when a waitress in a coffee shop asks, *"Miruku iremasu-ka"* (Do you want milk?). Some people will not feel any particular displeasure at these forms, but those who expect to be treated as superiors rather than equals — as in the forms *Nani-ni nasaimasu-ka*, *Nani-ni itashimashoo-ka* (What will you have) or *Miruku-o oire-itashimashoo-ka*, *Miruku-wa ikaga-desu-ka* (Would you like milk?) — will be irritated. Thus it is not enough to add *-masu* in order to be polite and indicate one's respect for the listener.

To summarize, we have seen in an examination of expressions of respect, how people are called, and the use of *sayoonara*, that the higher-lower distinction plays a major role in the structure of the Japanese language, its vocabulary, and the way words are used. But although we can by no means ignore this higher-lower distinction, it is doubtful whether it is the fundamental principle in terms of which everything in Japanese society is ordered. As touched upon in the previous section, in the Japanese concern toward relative human relations, and in humbling oneself and building up the other, lies the suggestion of another basic distinction, that of insiders and outsiders.

INTERACTING WITH OTHERS IN TERMS OF INNER-OUTER RELATIONS

The inner-outer distinction

In a Japanese company the section chief, or *kachoo*, is usually called *kachoo-san*. However, it is a mistake to tell someone on the telephone, *Kachoo-san-wa irasshaimasen* (The section chief isn't here): one is not supposed to use the respectful forms *kachoo-san* and *irassharu* to someone outside the company. The section chief has not become lower in terms of the higher-lower distinction, but the inner-outer distinction has been added. This rule also applies to talking about one's family at work. No matter how much one may respect one's father, one should not refer to him to a superior as *otoosan*: one should instead use the neutral form *chichi*. One's family is the smallest and most firmly established "inside" unit, and those who are not conscious of that when speaking to those outside the boundaries of the family are not regarded as full-fledged members of Japanese society. Training in this distinction begins in elementary school, and as students enter junior and senior high school, they are increasingly judged by their grasp of this inner-outer distinction in their language use.

In this way, the higher-lower distinction, present in honorific and humble forms such as *otoosan* for *chichi* and *kachoo-san* for *kachoo*, is not the sole consideration in Japanese language use; we must also consider the inner-outer distinction. And this inner-outer distinction is not a physical division but a psychological one; the individual is at the center and everything felt to belong inside is "inner" and everything falling outside is "outer." Consequently, the outer is defined differently at different times, and at times the gap between the inner and the outer is perceived as so great that everyone outside is regarded as nonhuman. In this sense, it might be more appropriate to use the term *yoso*, meaning stranger, rather than *soto*, meaning outside; and there are in fact a number of expressions in Japanese using *yoso* — *yoso-e iku* (to leave), *yosoyuki-no kimono* (one's best clothes, one's Sunday clothes), and *yoso-yososhii* (distant, cold, formal, standoffish).

The "inner" boundary is indicated in many ways. One is through the use of *san*. Therefore, when I heard an American student refer to an article by Edwin O. Reischauer in a seminar, saying *Raishawaa-san-no ronbun-dewa . . .* (in Mr. Reischauer's article . . .), I thought he had some personal relationship with Professor Reischauer. But he seemed too young for that. Since there was a difference of thirty or forty years in their ages, I thought perhaps they were relatives. I speculated in this way because the Japanese use *san* to indicate the existence of some relationship with that person. Of course *san* may also be used for well-known political figures whom one does not know directly, such as the former prime ministers of Japan Ohira-san and Fukuda-san; but in general, if someone attaches *san* to a name, the Japanese will assume that the speaker has a fairly close relationship with that person.

When I checked with this American student later, it turned out that he did not have any particular relationship with Reischauer. After I told him that in that case it was strange to say Reischauer-san, he changed this to Reischauer-sensee, but I had to tell him that using *sensee* sounds strange too. It is true that the Japanese will sometimes use *sensee*, as in Suzuki-sensee or

Ogawa-sensee, when referring to someone from whose writings they have learned much and whom they therefore regard as their teacher, even though they have not directly studied under him. However, *sensee*, like *san*, in most cases presupposes some direct relationship. In a seminar, it is more common to drop all such respect terms and simply say *Raishawaa-no ronbun-dewa* . . . (in Reischauer's article).

The atmosphere in that seminar was rather formal and the topics discussed were quite abstract; the relationships among the participants were also rather stiff. In that situation, to say Reischauer-shi would also resemble saying *sensee* and suggest some relationship with or a certain attitude toward Professor Reischauer.

Senpai, koohai

Other expressions are also used by the Japanese to indicate the relations between the speaker and other persons, and to finely distinguish whether one is an insider or an outsider and, if an insider, whether one is in the innermost circle or in the circle or two outside that. For example, all Japanese are accustomed to thinking in terms of *senpai* (literally, before-people) and *koohai* (literally, after-people), i.e., those who enter your school, company, or other group before or after you. These terms are relative to the speaker, with persons in the two categories receiving completely different treatment. These *senpai-kohai* categories are further subdivided into units of one year, and foreigners are often surprised by how differently *senpai* separated by only one year will be treated. Again, there is a considerable difference in the treatment of a *senpai* five years ahead of one and a *senpai* ten years ahead of one.

In this way many finely differentiated boundaries are drawn. Extremely stated, the Japanese divide the world into concentric rings moving outward from the innermost one of the immediate family to that of one's friends, one's region, and Japan — a way of thinking clearly reflected in, and in turn reinforced by, the Japanese language.

'Tomodachi' and 'friend'

The word "friend" in English has certain age restrictions, but these are much more pronounced for the Japanese *tomodachi*; *tomodachi* is used for those in one's own age group. Also, in Japan friendships tend to develop naturally in the midst of being thrown together and having the same experiences, rather than from an active effort to make friends. While Japanese schoolteachers may tell their students to make good friends or look for good friends, they seem to mean looking for good friends among those one meets every day rather than searching out new friends. I myself felt it rather strange when an American Japanologist about twenty years older than me called me *tomodachi* when introducing me to someone in Japanese. Of course I was glad he considered me his friend; but with the large difference in our ages, I wondered if he was using *tomodachi* in its Japanese meaning or in the meaning of the English "friend."

We can see a tendency in English, too, to use "friend" for those in one's own generation, but it can also be used for those considerably older or younger. Thus, in just these two words "friend" and "*tomodachi*," we can see the different expectations and use of language in English and Japanese.

The group formed by being in the same place at the same time

This Japanese classification of people into concentric rings, and using language accordingly, is typified by the creation of groups formed by being in the same place at the same time.

For example, three or four students are gathered together talking. If their teacher should come walking down the hall, they would be likely to say *Yamada-ga kita-zo* (Hey, Yamada's coming) rather than the more respectful *Sensee-ga irasshatta-yo* (The teacher is coming). Here we are not concerned with which expression is correct and should be used; the main point is that in this case — where the students recognize each other in a group and where their teacher suddenly appears outside of hearing distance of their voices — the teacher down the hall is outside the bounds of the student group. Consequently, such expressions as *Yamada-ga kita-zo* or *Sensee-ga kita, sensee-ga kita* (The teacher's coming, the teacher's coming) are not unusual.

This phenomenon is not limited to students and teachers. In various situations in everyday life, we find used, along with the respectful *Itoo-san-ga irasshatta-yo*, such plain forms as *Itoo-san kita-yo* (Mr./Ms. Ito has come), about someone for whom one ought to use respectful forms. The people together in one spot make up a group, and in most cases any person judged to be outside the bounds of that group will not be fully recognized by them. And the group thus formed is by no means simply a matter of physical proximity; it is also based on their mutual sanctioning and recognition of one another.

For example, if three people are talking together and a person comes who is an acquaintance of one of them, that new person will usually be ignored by the others. Or, if not ignored, that new person is gradually assimilated into the group, with his or her presence acknowledged and participation in the conversation permitted. In Western countries, a newly appearing fourth person is introduced to the others by his or her acquaintance and then verbally indicates a desire to participate in the group. In a Japanese group, on the other hand, it is all right for the new person to sit without saying anything at all. Merely sitting facing the others is the starting point in Japan; one gradually comes to feel comfortable in the group and starts entering the conversation. And taking part in a conversation in Japan is not limited to talking in words. Participation through one's facial expression or through giving *aizuchi* is also possible.

A group psychologically formed in this way displays a characteristic language behavior. Once the group boundaries have formed around the three or more people present, those within these boundaries will be considerate of each other's feelings and concentrate on enjoying themselves within the group. As a result, people nearby, but outside the group, are ignored. Thus a group made up of several individuals, or the members of a tour group, will talk or sing together in loud voices without any regard whatsoever for the other passengers in a train or bus; the group borders serve to make them blind to the presence of anyone outside the group.

There is an interesting Japanese expression which serves to confirm the existence of this situational group: *Koko-dake-no hanashi-da-ga* (literally, It is talk of only here). In this case "here" is of course not a physical place, but rather indicates the human relationship supported by being together in one spot. Conversation is carried out one-to-one, but this expression — that a conversation is for only the two people here — is a revealing one.

Further, as mentioned in Chapter 3, Japanese company men posted overseas spend many hours meeting with others personally to talk over business matters; and inside Japan as well, people often meet in coffee shops or the like to discuss some matter rather than taking care of it on the telephone. This behavior also demonstrates the importance of the bond formed by physically being together in one place.

And there are distinctive rules regarding leaving that situational group, as well as entering it. As someone simply present with others is regarded as participating in the group even if not actively talking, it is extremely difficult for the Japanese to tell another, "I want to talk with this person so please go over there and leave us alone for a few minutes." Similarly, the Japanese feel a strong resistance toward leaving the situational group ahead of the others. Americans and other foreigners feel free to tell the others and go if they want to or have to leave early for some reason, but this is extremely difficult for the Japanese to do. This problem is worthy of further investigation.

THE INNER-OUTER PHILOSOPHY AND THE STRONG TENDENCY TOWARD HARMONY AND UNITY

"Aitsu-wa 'rashiku nai' "

Once the boundaries of a group are established, the thinking that all within a group should think and act the same way comes to the surface. In certain cases, this process starts with denying the existence of individual differences; if such differences should exist, the pressure to become like the others becomes coercive in form. Such pressure can be seen in expressions frequently used toward new members of a group such as *rashiku nai* (not suitable, not like a _____) or *hoka-no hito-no yoo-ni yaru* (Do as other people do). In other cases, the new members attempt to become the same through assimilating to the others.

Superiority and inferiority complexes are present

behind both this coercion toward others and efforts to become the same as the others, leading at times to friction in communication. In general, however, an effort is made to find an average mean or other compromise and to avoid any friction. As a result, the typical pattern occurs of all in a Japanese group doing the same thing in the same way and with the same attitude.

'What will you have?' — 'What's good?'

This assimilation to others is not just a matter of language alone: it is often pointed out that the Japanese even have a characteristic way of ordering when they eat out together. Namely, they often all order the same thing rather than ordering according to their individual likes and dislikes, a phenomenon difficult for foreigners to understand.

Of course, this pattern depends on the personal relationships of the people involved, and not all Japanese will order the same thing. In close relationships, not much attention will be paid to what the others order. When an insider relationship has not yet been formed, however, all pay careful attention to what the others are having. And an insider relationship is not determined by the extent of social intercourse between those persons alone, but is also controlled by such factors as the atmosphere of the place, by what comes before and after the meal, and by the purpose of the meeting.

Thus, if an insider consciousness exists for a group of people, they will freely tell the waiter what they want and end up ordering different things. But if that insider consciousness is lacking, each will wonder aloud what would be good and sound out the others on what they would like until a consensus is reached and all order the same thing. Of course, sometimes an individual does not have any particular favorite, or does not want to bother picking something out of a wide choice, and so just orders what someone else is having; but it can hardly be considered accidental when five or ten people all order the same meal. This seems to be an interesting phenomenon in the eyes of many foreigners, particularly Americans and Europeans.

'Please treat me the same as before (even though I've become the section chief)'

When a new person enters an "insider" category, various characteristic patterns of linguistic behavior occur. One typical example is when a newly appointed superior enters a workplace from outside or is promoted from within the company. Most Japanese taking their post as a newly appointed section chief will express a desire to be treated the same as those now under them. If that new appointee has had some previous connection with them, he will try to impress on them his membership in the group through talking about shared experiences in the past, or searching for common points in his previous and new job duties. If he has been promoted from within the group, he will greet the others with something like "I haven't changed a bit from before and I want you to treat me as one of you." It would be very exceptional to greet them by saying, "I am your superior now and will be giving you orders."

In contrast with that, Americans, with some individual differences, tell their new work force in effect, "I'm your boss now and you should follow my orders." They also try to get their compliance by explaining that in return for following instructions, they will try to make correct judgments and issue appropriate directions. Or they may explain their particular philosophy and say it should work to everyone's benefit. I once worked for an American educational institution in Japan, and when a new director was appointed, he sent a letter several pages long to all the employees there before he arrived from the United States. In it, he explained his policies and requested our support of them.

Departing somewhat from the verbal for a moment, I have also been interested to observe that the attitude of Americans after being appointed to some job or office is also quite different from that of the Japanese. For example, when the Japanese select class officers at school or representatives in some group, those chosen will usually act and speak, as did the section chief mentioned above, in a way so as not to be separated from the rest of the group. Taking on a special attitude as a class officer or group representative will not be favorably regarded by most Japanese. Among Americans, on the other hand, someone chosen as the head of a group will make an active effort to show that he or she is the head. For example, when a boss is chosen in a Western, he will start to act like a boss. Once I saw a group of around twenty American students choose a committee chairman to organize some event. I was surprised to see that chairman stand up in front of them to open the meeting taking a stance with feet spread, hands on hips, and chest out. I had often seen this sort of pose in Westerns in my student days but had thought it was nothing more than a theatrical convention.

'Is that an order?'

The role of leader in Japan puts primary stress on overall coordination, and secondary stress on giving directions and leading others; but Americans reverse this emphasis, as can be observed in several common expressions. As pointed out before, Americans are, in a sense, very fond of orders — and by this I do not mean that only persons who have become leaders like orders and have to give them. In American movies, the expression "Is that an order?" often appears, a phrase little heard in the Japanese workplace. If someone were to say this in Japan, it would signal a very grave situation and, indeed, presage a crisis in worker-management relations. The Japanese also may ask this in jest, but it seems that Americans rather routinely ask whether something is an order or not. And we must also note their acceptance, or rather expectation, of being given orders.

We can thus say that in American society both those giving and receiving orders are fond of orders, although this way of giving orders does not imply that some persons are completely under the control of others. The Japanese, on the other hand, have an abhorrence of the word *meeree*, or "order." Japanese teachers teaching Americans will thus avoid giving orders and expect self-governing instead. But they may well be criticized by their American students for not performing all the duties of a teacher.

'Sore-o yatte-moraenai-kanaa'

Broadly speaking, the Japanese greatly dislike such words as "order" (*meeree*), "direction" (*shiji*), and "guidance" (*shidoo*). Therefore, those in positions of leadership must give much thought as to how to make their guidance effective. Of course, one will not have to take such pains if the matter is not so important and will not at all damage the honor, or work to the disadvantage, of the other, for example doing some routine paperwork or fetching something.

One must be more cautious, however, when the matter involves the listener's intentions and judgment. When a subordinate presents some proposal and asks whether it is satisfactory, one usually cannot come right out and say that it is no good. Of course, here too individual differences are found, but generally indirect expressions will be used. For example, the pattern . . . *kashira*, one added to a sentence to mean "I wonder if

. . .", is often thought of as one used primarily by women, but actually men also use it quite often. When a female worker asks if something is all right, her boss might say *Sore-de daijoobu-kashira* (I wonder if that is all right). In most cases, that really means, "That's no good. Do it over." And a superior will not give an order in the form "Please do this" (*Kore-o shite-kudasai*), but will say "I wonder if you could do such and such for me" (*Nani-nani shite-moraenai-kanaa* or *Nani-nani moraenai-daroo-kanaa*), and will preface this request with *Taihen mooshiwake nai-n-da-keredo* (literally, I have no way to apologize to you for it but . . .) or *Gokuroo-dakeredomo* (I am sorry to put you to this trouble but . . .).

This indirect form of expression is due to the Japanese dislike of appearing to disregard the listener by giving some instruction in a clear and definite form or, in other words, a dislike of forcing oneself and one's wishes onto the other. In a situation where it is particularly difficult to give instructions or orders, a Japanese will not use verbal means alone but will try to persuade and lead through other means as well, such as changing the location and perhaps going out drinking with the others.

The higher-lower distinction is not fundamental

If we think in terms of concentric rings of human relations, the superior and his subordinates are located in different rings. That is, the rank and file of employees comprise one large ring or group, and their superior is outside of it. Accordingly, although he has the higher social position, when he issues orders relying on that position, the strong possibility exists that the organization will not function smoothly. A superior should rather guide his subordinates by taking on the appearance, or achieving the reality, of entering inside the employee group and being equal and one with those inside, striving for a good understanding of their wishes.

In this sense, we can consider the drives toward harmony and unity within the group as prior to the higher-lower distinction in Japanese society. In contrast, in the United States, the higher-lower distinction clearly has precedence. Accordingly, both those who give orders and those who take them willingly accept this distinction as the basic pattern for behavior. This constitutes a major difference between these two countries.

Generalizing from these few examples is a large leap, but at the very least we can say that Japanese culture and the Japanese way of thinking is not fundamentally based on higher and lower relations; Japan is not a vertical society characterized by primarily vertical relationships. Rather, the pull and responsiveness toward lateral relations is the fundamental dynamic in Japan, and the Japanese are imbued with the desire for leveling and equalization due to their strong drive toward harmony and unity. We can thus say that higher-lower relations are the surface appearance, or *tatemae*, and lateral relations the real essence, or *honne*. (The lateral referred to here involves the creation of the insider boundaries and the intense drive for harmony and unity within these boundaries.)

Further, it is only speculation on my part, but I believe that in Japanese society the lateral relationships, namely those working for equality, are fundamental, and, in order to enable the society to function smoothly as a whole, the higher-lower system was imposed as the surface reality (*tatemae*). In contrast, in most European and American countries, vertical relationships, such as the parent-child relationship, are fundamental. Since these societies are premised on vertical relationships resulting in a clear distinction between those spurring others on and those spurred on, the lateral element is added to make the system functional.

In vertical relationships, the differences between the two parties become crystal clear. Precisely because Western societies are premised on the existence of such a difference, a philosophy is needed to abstract that difference and attempt to make the society just. Isn't that what the concepts of democracy, liberty, or equality are? Democracy was introduced into Japan by the Americans in the postwar period, but it is only natural that American democracy did not take root in Japan. For Japan has its own Japanese form of democracy, in which groups with firm borders are set up and relations within those groups are fundamentally equal.

Chapter 6. Changes in the Life and Language of the Contemporary Japanese

CHANGES IN THE CONTENT OF COMMUNICATION
— Internationalization and standardization —

Changes in the listener

The special characteristics of spoken Japanese discussed in the previous chapters are not in evidence for every situation and every type of human relationship. As in other languages, Japanese speakers have a certain amount of freedom as to how to express a given fact, emotion, or situation. Further, language is inseparable from the life of its speakers, and extra-linguistic elements inevitably exert an influence on the use and structure of language. We must never forget that language is a living entity, not something rigidly fixed and immobile.

Consequently, in thinking about what the Japanese language should ideally be like, or how it should be taught, it is essential to grasp how it is used in practice for communication, examining the actual conditions and problems of language use today. If we roughly define the factors in the actual use of language for communication, a giver and receiver of some message are most fundamental of all. Interposed between these are the conditions, means, and content of what is being communicated; and these elements are conceived of here as general societal phenomena or constructs for analysis, rather than as elements in any particular communication.

What was communicated by the Japanese in the

past? What were the special characteristics and the physical limitations of their language behavior? When we think about who an average Japanese a generation ago would have been likely to talk to, it is evident that those possible language partners were from a much more limited pool than is available to a Japanese today. Of course, even thirty years ago, some Japanese did move about within Japan and have many chances to speak with Japanese of different dialects, or did go abroad and talk with foreigners in Japanese. Their absolute numbers, however, were minuscule if compared to today. An average Japanese now is many, many times more likely to come into contact with a dialect-speaker, and even has a chance of speaking at some time with a foreigner in Japanese. And if we add in indirect exposure to widely varying speakers through television and radio, it is even clearer how far-reaching the changes have been.

The recent changes in transportation and means of communication have of course brought about changes in one's conversation partners, and these changes have in turn had a great impact on the language behavior of the Japanese; when we consider the inevitable changes in our lives in the years ahead, we must acknowledge that the Japanese language will continue to change in unforeseeable ways. The dizzying pace of change is evident if we simply consider that the physical distance between the peoples of the world will undoubtedly be shortened during the last half of this century as much, or more than, in the course of several centuries up to the beginning of the Meiji period in 1868.

'Watashi-wa ane-o motte-imasu'

The contact with foreigners and foreign culture did not, of course, start in the 1970s and 1980s. Since the beginning of the Meiji period in 1868, foreign languages, especially English, have come to be taught to all the Japanese, and as a result a flood of borrowed words and expressions translated word for word have appeared in Japanese. Many of these loan words are used in ways and meanings completely different from their original language; two examples of Japanese English incomprehensible to native English-speakers are *sarariiman* ("salary man," company man) and *beesu-uppu* ("base up," a raise of the basic wage rate). Other expressions born out of the contact with English include translated expressions, such as . . . *suru-ya ina-ya* . . . (as soon as one (does something)), and constructions such as the passive used with the object of an action as the subject.

This process of new Japanese patterns being formed under the influence of other languages seems, if anything, to be accelerating today. One major cause of this is the use in compulsory junior and senior high school English classes of dubious and clumsy Japanese sentences that would never occur naturally in conversation, such as *"Watashi-wa ane-o motte-imasu"* (I have an (older) sister; more naturally *Ane-ga imasu*) and *"Kare-wa kare-no imooto-ni issatsu no hon-o ataemashita"* (He gave a book to his (younger) sister; more naturally *Imooto-ni hon-o agemashita*). All too often no consideration is given to whether or not these are appropriate as Japanese sentences or even whether or not they are accurate as translations of English sentences.

Recently the dubbing of foreign television shows has improved considerably and unnatural places are no longer so noticeable, but extra words unnecessary in Japanese conversation still appear due to the necessity of supplying words whenever the mouths of the American actors and actresses are moving and the like. Typical of those unnatural usages are terms for referring to others, with *anata* (you) and *watashi* (I) appearing much more often than usual. And strangely enough, expressions that sounded odd when dubbing first began have gradually come to sound natural; it seems that a convention has been established that this is what dubbed Japanese should be like.

A different Japanese has also developed in Hawaii. When I listened to the Japanese radio broadcasts there, *naniwabushi* recitations started from 6 a.m. with funeral notices interspersed. Interesting as a cultural phenomenon, these broadcasts were also interesting linguistically. The Japanese used by Japanese-Americans in panel discussions and by the disc jockeys had a strong international flavor; they liberally mixed English and Japanese, as in *"Nekusuto Satadee-wa, tokubetsu-seeru-o ____ honten-de itashimasu"* (Next Saturday there will be a special sale at the main branch of the ____ store). "A strong international flavor" is a favorable way of describing this; but at the same time, we have to admit that some indefinable loss has also taken place.

The loss of the Japanese linguistic inheritance

The Japanese language is undergoing great changes within Japan as well. Although there are now a considerable number of programs in regional dialects on television, perhaps in an effort to appeal to a wider range of viewers, standard Japanese (originally the Tokyo dialect) is spreading throughout Japan. Even in Osaka, a traditionally strong rival of Tokyo which has resolutely protected its own dialect, recent subway announcements have been in standard Japanese. Osakans have not lost pride in their own culture; but as many people from different backgrounds gather there, the pressure to use a nationally accepted speech style has been increasing. Unlike older Kansai residents, young people are now frequently unsure about how they should speak to those coming from other areas in Japan, whether they should use the Kansai dialect or something approximating the Tokyo dialect. In a related development, an increasing number of young people have difficulty answering questions about accent and usage in the Osaka and Kyoto dialects. Not a few have to stop and think when asked whether they say ha̅-na or ha̅-na for hana (花 ; flower).

The diversification of language users brings about the collision and mixing of different language systems. In the absence of any deep concern about language and an unremitting effort to prevent it, language will seek a common value, drifting in different directions; it is easy for all to be satisfied with that which fills the needs of the moment. The situation of language in a village society, where an extremely limited set of speakers and listeners have been born, lived out their lives, and died in the same place, is by no means the same as in our highly mobile society today where endless change in conversation partners is possible. In the latter situation, standardization of the language is inevitable.

Standardization is certainly desirable in many ways. No one will deny that it is better to avert such tragedies as the suicide of young people who come to Tokyo from northeastern Japan to look for jobs and form an inferiority complex about their accent. In that sense, the steady advance toward standardization is a positive development. At the same time, however, the Japanese must guard against losing a major share of the Japanese linguistic inheritance, against tending to ignore the emotional in a stress upon the transmission of the factual, and against falling into the expedient under the pressure of the presence of heterogeneous elements.

Another area to be watched with concern is how the

special characteristics of spoken Japanese supported by the "insider" culture will function and develop in the midst of these changes in the content of communication.

THE MEANS AND ENVIRONMENT OF COMMUNICATION
— Changes in life style —

A day spent without talking

One night I was startled to get a very late telephone call from a friend; it turned out that he didn't have any special reason for calling, but had suddenly felt very lonely when he realized that he hadn't really talked to anyone all day. When I thought about it, I realized that, as my friend's experience indicated, talking is no longer so necessary in our everyday life today. Particularly those who live alone may get up, wash their faces, look through the newspaper, leave their room, and go to a small neighborhood restaurant for breakfast without exchanging a single word with anyone. At the restaurant one will be greeted on entering, but no response is necessary. To order, one can simply say *"Teeshoku"* for a set breakfast; and unless one is friendly with the proprietor, that one word is all that is necessary.

Next one takes the train to work. Tickets are now sold by vending machine so there is no need to give a destination to the station employee at the window — and most workers have commuter passes making even this step unnecessary. No words are exchanged at the ticket gate, and all those packed around one in the rush-hour trains are strangers unless one should happen to run into an acquaintance and call out a greeting. One simply listens passively to the names of the stations being announced over the loudspeaker until one arrives at work. Here someone at the reception area may greet you, but in most cases one proceeds on to one's own work area without saying anything; many enter by punching a time clock. Those who tend a machine obviously do not have to say anything to that machine. Even if a superior making the rounds addresses one, usually only a few words are required in response, and the content of many jobs is so fixed that few instructions will be received from others. At the many places which are automated, one silently works or watches machinery work until lunch time.

At the lunch hour one is likely to go to a company dining hall. In the system in effect at most large companies, one buys a token from a vending machine, sits down at a table, and gives it to a waiter or waitress. In a self-service cafeteria system, no one even comes and asks you what you want. After lunch, work proceeds in silence as before until the day is done. You leave work and enter a coffee shop. There the one word "Coffee" is sufficient. You return home and watch TV. Certainly a stream of words pours out from the set, but no normal person talks with it. Then your favorite programs end or you get tired of the noise and you are shocked to realize that you haven't really talked with anyone all day.

This scenario is all too likely in one of today's big cities. Even if the situation is not quite this extreme, as automation and mechanization increase, opportunities to use language steadily decrease. For example, customers regularly exchanged words with the keepers of small stalls selling fish or vegetables, but there is no real chance of conversation with the clerks at a supermarket checkout. At the most, one might ask where some merchandise is located or about a price.

This forlorn state of affairs makes for a lonely life. Perhaps in response, talking vending machines have recently been introduced. When you put your money in some cigarette machines now, a taped voice says in Japanese, "Thank you very much. Cigarettes make a convenient present," as your change and cigarettes come out. A taped voice also calls out *"Irasshai"* (Welcome) at some supermarkets when you come in and *"Maido arigatoo-gozaimasu"* (Thank you very much) when you leave. But these taped messages are a sorry substitute for an exchange of words with a real, live flesh-and-blood person.

No letters written all year but New Year's cards

Another important factor in revolutionizing Japanese language behavior has been the spread of the telephone — and the rate of telephone use is moving steadily upward. Recently, not only does each family have a telephone, but more and more families have extension phones as well.

No one can deny the many advantages of the telephone: one can easily talk with someone without the time-consuming process of writing a letter, one can make oneself understood more exactly, emotional elements difficult to express in writing are easy to convey through one's voice, it is far faster than a letter or telegram, and it permits the exchange of information with the listener.

Thus, it is not altogether surprising if young people today do not write letters. And it is not just young people who do not write letters; a surprisingly large number of the Japanese today write nothing in the course of a year but New Year's cards. In passive language activity as well, means of communication based on elements other than writing have become central in Japanese life. The deep penetration of radio and television into the daily life of the Japanese people has excluded writing that much more from their lives. Although characters do appear quite often on television in newscasts and the like, it is primarily a medium of sound and pictures.

A language life without writing

Among publications as well, those centered on pictures rather than written characters, such as the story comic books read by adults as well as children, are dominant today. Ten years or so ago letters to the editor deplored the then new sight of university students reading comic books in the trains, but now one can see many elite organization men reading comic books written for children. The waiting rooms at barbershops and doctor's offices, which until a few years ago were largely stocked with picture magazines similar to the American *Life* and *Look* and other weekly magazines, are now filled with comic books. In coffee shops as well, the reading material provided for customers largely consists of adult and juvenile comic books. This shift in the means of conveying information seems to fulfill Marshall McLuhan's predictions of twenty years ago, or even surpass them.

What exactly is the significance of a language life not based on written characters? This is a topic fully worthy of debate and study, but the situation at present — with the changes in the means of communication, the spread of the telephone, and the development and routinization of visual means of communication — is in a state of such flux that it cannot be fully analyzed as yet. Under such conditions, it is difficult to know how to best study language behavior: what role is played by the auditory, what is the relationship between the visual and language, and what position should be given to written characters?

The effects of the trend toward the nuclear family

To turn momentarily from the strictly linguistic,

the recent trend toward the nuclear family has been the subject of much debate in Japan. The Japanese are unsure what sort of human relationships will be produced by the weakening of traditional family ties and how the roles of parent and child will change.

The Japanese language originally developed in the situation of people living together in an extended family system. When a grandfather and grandmother, a married couple, and their children all lived in the same house, one might address anyone from grandchildren to grandparents; language use was thus premised on paying attention to the differing relationships within a group made up of over four or five people.

The concern with people's relative status, as seen in the respect language, was fostered by, and became fixed in, this sort of family configuration. Now, however, the family grouping is changing to the smaller nuclear family, and the housing of that nuclear family is changing from the Japanese-style residence, where the whole family essentially lives in one large room divided up by sliding paper screens, to a Western-style residence with separate rooms for each individual. With these fundamental changes in family structure and form of housing, changes are also inevitable in the language used to speak to others and in the expressions reflecting the attitude of the speaker.

The characteristic Japanese trend toward harmony and uniformity discussed in Chapter 4 will undoubtedly be greatly influenced by these changes. It is relatively easy for someone who has shared the same experiences to infer what others are thinking or what they have done in the past. When, however, one lives in a separate house or a separate room, the finding of common experience becomes more difficult. Under these circumstances, it is only natural to expect a radical decline in *omoiyari*, a consideration toward others, or, rather, in the ability to guess what others are thinking and feeling.

What influence will these changes in life style, especially in Japanese housing, have on the tendency toward harmony and unity, on the concern with relative human relationships, and on "insider-outsider" thinking? It is impossible to be sure, but they will undoubtedly be a major factor in the dying out of many of the special characteristics of spoken Japanese described in the earlier chapters of this book.

One example of this is the familiar complaint that recently people do not give proper greetings, a matter also discussed earlier. The customary greetings enforced by life in an extended family seem to have been lost with the shift to the nuclear family and to individual rooms in housing. However, if we think about it, this seems to be a somewhat paradoxical development: when people are independent and living separately, greetings when they meet should become more, not less, important. The required greetings in Western society are, after all, premised on individuals having different personalities and different ways of thinking. What is the significance, then, of the decrease in greetings in Japan? Perhaps Japanese language behavior is now in a transitional period, as is the Japanese life style.

At any rate, the processes mentioned above — mechanization and automation bringing about a life without words, changes in means of communication leading to a life without writing, and changes in life style influencing greetings and other verbal expressions — are obviously advancing rapidly in Japanese society today. From a different perspective, these changes can also be considered in terms of the urbanization of rural society or of the shift from a territorial or kinship society to a profit society.

At the present time, it is impossible to fully estimate the dimensions of the change in language brought about by these violent changes in society. Another important topic of consideration is how the Japanese themselves, and the language they use, can play an autonomous role in that changing society.

THE CONTENT AND MEANS OF COMMUNICATION

Why is *ame* 'rain' in English?

There are two major elements in respect to the formation of a language and its vocabulary. One is arbitrariness and the other efficiency.

To take up the arbitrary nature of language first, children exposed to English often ask, "Why is *ame* called 'rain' in English?" Their parents are troubled for an answer and will say something like, "Why . . . it just is, that's all." Water falling from the sky is called *ame* in Japanese and "rain" in English; when the temperature is low and it crystallizes and becomes white, it is then called *yuki* in Japanese and "snow" in English. However, there is nothing in the words *ame* or "rain" that has any natural relationship with the physical phenomenon itself. In the same way, although the same succession of sounds with a different accent will mean rain or the gelatin-like food *ame* (written with a different Chinese character from the *ame* meaning rain), there is no natural or inevitable relationship between *ame* with the first syllable pronounced higher meaning rain and *ame* with the second syllable higher meaning the food. However, if someone therefore decides to use *yuki* in place of *ame* for rain, no one will understand this. Within any given language, words are decided societally, and no single individual can change the form of a given word because it seems unsuitable. As the same applies to "rain" and "snow" in English, the only answer one can give to the question, "Why does one say *ame* in Japanese and 'rain' in English?", is that these words are used because of a societal agreement to do so.

Within any language system, not only the vocabulary is agreed upon societally, but also the pronunciation and grammar. Thus an individual cannot, for example, unilaterally change the sentence *"Eki-no chikaku-ni hon'ya-ga arimasu"* (There is a bookstore near the station) into *"Hon'ya-ga chikaku-ni eki-no arimasu"* (a meaningless sentence), and the meaning will also be changed if one says *Chikaku-ni eki-no hon'ya-ga arimasu* (There is a station bookstore nearby). The set order of words will vary according to the language, and in principle no way of ordering is more rational than any other.

However, the rationality or efficiency of a language in actual use can become a problem. What particular physical reality is indicated by *ame* and *yuki* respectively is decided societally; but when one sees something falling from the sky, a personal judgment and selection of words is required to decide whether to say *"Aa, ame-da"* (Oh, it's raining) or *"Aa, yuki-da"* (Oh, it's snowing). If one says *ame* even though *yuki* is falling, you are, intentionally or unintentionally, misrepresenting the facts. One may physically mistake *yuki* for *ame*, say *yuki* although you meant to say *ame*, or intentionally lie and say *yuki*, but all of these are inappropriate.

The selection between *ame* and *yuki* is also difficult when what is falling is something between rain and snow. Luckily the word *mizore* (sleet) exists for that situation. A stock of vocabulary and sentence patterns sufficient to express any situation as the occasion demands is indispensable for a society. However, the number of functional words in a language is limited, and those understood by only a restricted number of people will be meaningless as a common asset of that society. Consequently, in any one society, a bias will naturally develop in the general vocabulary and types of sentence patterns. In this way, X society may be rich in vocabulary concerning animals, while Y society differentiates between many different grasses and trees.

The stress on factual matters or human relationships

One day I asked an American graduate student to write as many English sentences as possible from the Japanese sentence, *Itta-to iimashita* (He said he went). He wrote about twenty sentences right away by changing the "said" part of the sentence, as in

    He said that he went.
    He told me that he went.
    He commented that he went.
    He stated that he went.
    He claimed that he went., etc.

He said that if he had more time to think about it, there were probably as many as one-hundred variants. Then he started on the "went" part of the sentence:

    He said that he went.
    He said that he has gone.
    He said that he had gone., etc.

Changing both parts of the sentence, he came up with

    He has said that he went.
    He has said that he has gone.

Soon he had a whole sheet of paper covered with possible sentences.

The next day I showed the English sentence "He said that he went" to a Japanese and asked him to write all the possible corresponding Japanese sentences. He started with *"Kare-ga itta-to kare-wa iimashita"* so I asked him to write only sentences that would occur naturally in speech. He continued and wrote:

    Itta-to itta (both "go" and "say" in plain form).
    Itta-to iimashita ("say" in polite form).
    Itta-to osshaimashita ("say" in respectful form).
    Itta-to ii-yagatta ("say" in derogatory form).
    Itta-to nukashita ("say" in derogatory form).
    Irasshatta-to itta ("go" in respectful form).
    Irasshatta-to iimashita.
    Irasshatta-to osshatta (both in the respectful, plain form).
    Irasshatta-to osshaimashita.
    Iki-yagatta-to iimashita ("go" in derogatory form).
    Itte-shimatta-to iimashita (the finality of going stressed)., etc.

As this was nothing more than an experiment for my own personal interest, it is dangerous to generalize from the results. However, I was intrigued by the different concerns reflected in the answers of the American and the Japanese.

The American changed the sentence according to the content of the action of "say" and "go," that is, in relation to the facts of the matter, while the Japanese changed the human relationships. Although different ways of stating the content exist in Japanese as well, such as *noberu* (state) and *kataru* (tell), the Japanese did not use them. He may have been influenced by the word "said" being used in the English sentence he was given; but it would seem to be more than mere personal preference that, in contrast to this focusing on the human relations and attitude of the speaker, as in the plain, polite, and respectful forms for "say" (*itta, iimashita,* and *osshatta*), the American first made changes in the content, as in "say," "tell," "speak," and "state," and then shifted to different tenses, as in "went," "has gone," and so forth. Their respective preferences are suggestive of the special characteristics of the Japanese language, of the characteristic Japanese use of language, and of what the Japanese want to convey to others in verbal communication.

A priority given to factual information

Each society differs in what kind of information its members want to convey and receive from others through language. At the same time there is also variation among individuals. X may regard the transfer of factual information as primary, while Y may want only a minimum of factual information and instead value communication of the speaker's psychological attitude toward and evaluation of persons or facts.

This personal difference between X and Y can also be thought of in terms of the group to which a person belongs. Engineers, for example, tend to fall into the X-type and poets into the Y-type; most businessmen tend toward the X-type and most housewives toward the Y-type. And even the same person will want to convey or obtain different sorts of information at different times. The main question here is what the predominant type of information being conveyed through language is for the Japanese society as a whole, and whether or not that is changing now.

Although it is easy to say "the predominant type of information," the actual reality is extremely complex and difficult to grasp. However, if we limit the discussion to this distinction between a concern for factual information and a concern for psychological attitude, as seen in the respect language, and if we take into account the present developments in means of transportation and communication and the accelerating pace of contacts between differing peoples, we can conclude that precedence is given to information concerning factual matters, and information about psychological attitude is clearly regarded as secondary.

Stated in this way, one might think that here is the cause of the decline in use of respect language, but such is not the case. It is true that special words like *asobasu* (to deign to do) and *haietsu* (an audience with the Emperor) are now little used, and abundant mistakes are regularly made in the use of the humble language. It is not reasonable, however, to expect a simplification of expressions revealing relative relationships at a time when human relationships are becoming ever more complex. A state of confusion now exists in regard to the respect language, and a reorganization and unification of forms is difficult. Even though there are cries of a breakdown of the respect language, little can be done as long as there is no overriding societal concern about correcting the situation.

Compared to that, the need for correct information and for improvement in the means of transmission of factual information is relatively clear, and this problem seems to be well on the way to solution. Information pours out from the world of economics, the industrial world, the political world, and the academic world, and computers are becoming larger and more complex to answer these needs. However, even if a computerized translation machine should become feasible, first precedence would undoubtedly be given to factual information, and matters concerning human psychology would receive short shrift.

Honjitsu kyuugyoo → *Honjitsu kyuugyoo-itashimasu*

The language used in signs and notices in Japanese shops has also changed recently. Formerly the sign *Honjitsu kyuugyoo* (Closed today) was used when a shop was closed for the day. If the sign was hanging there for two days in a row, one would simply think

"Ah, they're closed today too." But these days when a shop is closed for more than one day, the sign considerately reads "___ nichi-kara ___ nichi-made rinji-kyuugyoo-itashimasu" (We will be closed temporarily from ___ to ___). Sometimes the reason for the closing is also provided.

The use of the humble form *itashimasu*, indicating relative status, shows a stronger concern toward psychological attitude than toward facts. Rather than simply putting up the rather brusque *Honjitsu kyuugyoo*, this newer style of notice reflects the feelings of the person who put it up, a considerable change. We can also view this as one part of a general societal shift from the written language to the spoken language. In the change from *Honjitsu kyuugyoo* to *Honjitsu kyuugyoo-itashimasu*, we can see the formal tone of the written style giving way to the more personal appeal of the spoken language.

Individual differences in expectations of what should be communicated

In Chapter 4, I discussed a particular use of *gurai*, *hodo*, and *bakari* (about); I stated that an expression like *Ringo-o itsutsu-gurai* (Give me five apples; literally, about five apples) does not indicate four or five or six apples, but rather shows the psychological attitude of the buyer and, in effect, softens the demand. I also pointed out the social dimension of its use; the rate of use in urban apartment complexes, or *danchi*, is lower than in older, more traditional areas of the city, and many Japanese feel that there is no need for such vague expressions. Certainly, if one is only interested in precisely conveying the facts, this *gurai*, *hodo*, or *bakari* is unnecessary.

However, in actuality, a considerable percentage of the Japanese feel uncomfortable requesting something without *enryo*, or reserve, in their language. Clearly a conflict exists here between the information one wants to communicate and its expected linguistic form of expression, and we may conclude that a certain friction unconsciously occurs in such communication. The differing expectations of how a given communication should be expressed is a problem worthy of our attention.

'Kaettara denwa-shimasu'

We should pay as much attention to the means as to the content of communication. Naturally enough, the Japanese do not all use the same means of expression in verbal communication. This is not simply a problem of the choice of individual words or of differing styles. Rather, it concerns to what extent an individual values language itself and depends on words in communication.

The attitude, as in the ancient Japanese saying, that silence is a virtue is still very much alive in Japanese society today. At the very least, silent people are little criticized. If one does not answer when a reply is called for by the situation, it is a different matter, but not talking at some gathering will not be criticized by the others as a lack of sociability. In fact, someone who does not say a thing but sits there smiling will be regarded more favorably than someone who talks well, but leaves before the others do.

Individuals vary in how much they depend on words. Some people take care of their business in a few words and some use a great number of words, with many others falling somewhere in between these two extremes. People also vary in the extent to which they try to convey their thoughts and emotions through such extralinguistic elements as common experiences and knowledge, physical space, physical objects, attitude, and facial expression.

"*Kaettara denwa-shimasu*" (I'll call you when I get home) is an ordinary sentence in Japanese conversation. Even though who is returning, or where he or she is returning to, is not explicitly stated, in context it is clear that it is the speaker who is returning home. Similarly, it is understood that it is the speaker who will be doing the telephoning, although the subject here too is not explicitly stated. If we were to say the same sentence in English, however, we would have to supply the words "I," "home," and "I" even if they are understandable from the context.

In the same way, American speakers of Japanese tend to say something like "*Ocha-o doozo nonde-kudasai*" (Please drink the tea), as discussed earlier in this book. The Japanese will express this in the single word *Doozo* (Please) or in the phrase *Ocha-o doozo* (literally, Please, the tea); *nonde-kudasai* (please drink) is unnecessary. In Japanese, in contrast with English, it is appropriate to adopt a form of language behavior which makes oneself understood to the other through dependence on the situation. However, if we consider the range in form of expression found among the Japanese themselves, this seems to be too sweeping a judgment. When I visit different places, tea is generally served, and it seems to me that young people are now using a different level of politeness, with *Doozo onomi-kudasai* (Please drink it) becoming more frequent.

'*Kesa-wa taihen ii otenki-desu-keredomo . . .*'

Expressions relying on situational elements, especially on the evaluation and response of the listener, are, however, still very frequent in Japanese conversation. This sometimes leads to misunderstandings with foreigners. For instance, the following experience happened to a certain eminent American scholar of linguistics on one of her trips to Japan. She was invited by a

Japanese scholar she knew to stay at his family's home, and she was taking a bath when a member of the family came and said from the other side of the door, *"Tsuki-ga kiree-desu-yo. Yoroshikattara . . ."* (The moon is lovely tonight. If it is all right . . .). That American jumped out of the bath when she heard this because she thought for a moment that *Yoroshikattara* might mean *Yoroshikattara, haitte-mo ii-desu-ka* (Is it all right to come in?)! A Japanese hearing *Tsuki-ga kirei-desu-yo* (The moon is lovely tonight) could predict that this will be followed by something like "How about coming to look at it?" or "Won't you come look at it after finishing your bath?". However, this American scholar, in spite of her long study of Japanese culture and knowledge of the Japanese attitude to the moon, found herself reacting in an English-language way and leaping out of the tub.

Keredomo (but, although) is very popular in Japanese, as in the sentence, *"Kesa-wa taihen ii-tenki-desu-keredomo, kaijoo-no minasan yoku oatsumari-kudasai-mashita"* (The weather is very fine this morning, but all of you have kindly come to this meeting today). This construction is often used by television and radio announcers but is sometimes criticized because, strictly speaking, it should indicate some opposing or contradictory conditions. Native English-speakers also find the Japanese use of *keredomo*, its shortened form *kedo*, *ga* (but), and *shikashi* (however) difficult to understand. If the sentences using them are written down, anyone can see that they are often illogical. However, they crop up constantly in spoken Japanese and, except for times they appear in the mass media, little fault is found with them. The reason is that, rather than indicating a logical connection between clauses, these words primarily express one's psychological attitude toward the listener. Along with such words as *gurai*, *hodo*, and *bakari* (about), they indicate one's feelings of humility toward others. Thus, *shikashi* (however) is often used where, if one stops to think about it, there is no reason to say "however." If we consider the characteristic Japanese dependence on the situation and the importance of the relationship between the listener and the speaker, however, we will be able to understand the function of that *shikashi*.

As a means of verbal communication, Japanese is characterized by a high rate of dependence on the situation which is quite different from the mode of attempting to incorporate the content of the communication into the very forms of the language itself. Not only in communication between Japanese and foreigners but also among the Japanese themselves, individual differences exist and language behavior is in a state of considerable flux. In this way, these principal elements of factual information and information concerning psychological attitude in the realm of what is communicated, and the reliance on both words and the situational in the realm of how that is communicated, constitute important clues in examining and linking together the language and the life of the contemporary Japanese. This perspective is also important for inquiries into the most desirable form of language activity.

CHANGES IN THE SPEAKER

'The language of young people today . . .'

These days many changes in the Japanese themselves have been receiving much attention. Just physically, young people are larger, the average Japanese is taller, and average life expectancy is now one of the highest in the world. Of course the Japanese language has not changed directly because of these physical changes; there is little relationship between physical features and language. But we can say that the lengthening of life and the changes in language are not completely unrelated.

The Japanese often deplore the language used by young people, a complaint undoubtedly heard throughout the ages. Some change, however, has occurred in what is referred to by "young people," as we can see if we think about status in a given society, the expectations directed toward twenty-year-olds, and their societal role.

If the average life expectancy in a society is thirty years, then twenty-year-olds, fifty-year-olds, and seventy-year-olds will all clearly have a different importance. In that society, twenty-year-olds will bear the responsibilities and obligations of a full-fledged adult member of society; indeed, they may well do so even before they reach twenty. In ancient Japan, youths went through the *genpuku* rite marking the attainment of manhood before the age of fifteen, but the age of adulthood has gradually become later and later. At present, the transition to adulthood formally takes place at eighteen or twenty, revealing the societal changes that have taken place in status and responsibility.

As we have seen before, one basic criterion in the use of the Japanese language is the consideration of relative human relationships, a concern particularly striking in the respect language. When someone is the representative of a social group or family, the responsibility for a certain rate and type of greetings is quite clear. And the possibility of being the head or representative of a group or family is far greater for a twenty-year-old when the average life expectancy is thirty years than when it is fifty years. It is only natural in the former case for someone to be able to give adult greetings at an early age.

Thus, generally speaking, in today's world of the nuclear family and a life expectancy of seventy years, a twenty-year-old probably has living parents and grandparents, and will have many fewer opportunities to take responsibility and talk accordingly than when the life expectancy was thirty or fifty years. We must take a close look at the complaints about the poor language of young people today and see what areas of language are actually affected.

We should also take into account the extended period of schooling as a factor in the transformation of young people. The use of language in school life is clearly different from that in the general society. Probably everyone has noticed at some time or other the clear difference in the language of those who quit school and entered society after junior or senior high school and those who went on to college or graduate school. The increased opportunities for higher education have also had a considerable impact on the language used throughout Japanese society as a whole. The changes in composition of the various groups in Japanese society, in the ways of participating in those groups, and in the ways of thinking and responding as individuals have all had an effect on the changes in language usage and in language itself.

Changes in world view and language

We must also examine changes in how individuals view the world. Those world views may consist of various elements; some of these are how one views human beings, how one views inanimate objects and animals, and how one feels these should be treated. Of course the evaluation one has of language will also influence changes in language. Various other matters can be included in the world view held by individuals, but here I would like to talk about only the above attitudes toward humanity, objects, and language.

As I have touched upon here and there in this book, one of the special characteristics of Japanese behavior is the custom of thinking about others in terms of whether or not they are in one's group, i.e. whether they are insiders or outsiders. Also, as seen in Chapter 5, thinking about people in terms of the upper-lower distinction was quite strong in Japan in the prewar period but has now weakened; in fact, that upper-lower viewpoint can be thought of as essentially one part of the insider-outsider framework which was sometimes promoted for political or institutional reasons. Consequently, that distinction is subject to collapse. Presently this upper-lower distinction does exist as *tatemae*, or the surface reality; but in actuality the thinking opposed to that distinction is the one recognized in Japanese society today, and we must be fully aware of the doubts displayed about this higher-lower viewpoint. In contrast to that, the inner-outer or insider-outsider viewpoint is deeply rooted among the Japanese today, as can be seen at every turn.

The formation of the insider-outsider framework

Recently, whether a deliberate strategy on the part of teachers or not, quite free language such as would be used between friends, passes between the students and the teachers with no offense being taken. Nevertheless, when students directly address their teachers, they usually use respect language, a usage following the upper-lower criterion. When students are talking about a teacher, however, the dropping of respect language and terms of respect like *-sensee* or *-san* is usual. This would seem to be due to the teacher being considered outside the circle of students and being treated by them accordingly.

This insider-outsider boundary also exists among the students themselves, and even among junior high school students, strict respect language is customary toward students one or two years ahead. It is quite clear that the difference of only one year puts up a border between them.

As touched upon in many chapters in this book, this thinking in which one builds categories and treats human beings accordingly forms the foundation for the psychological structure of the Japanese people; it is so strong and deeply rooted that it seems almost constitutional and beyond change. This drawing up of boundaries is one sort of groupism and is self-evidently different from the manner of doing things in a society where individuality is more fundamental. On the other hand, a respect for individuality has been strengthened in some areas of Japanese school education and everyday life; and there has been a general trend toward the freedom of the individual, both societally and in the move toward the nuclear family and individual rooms in housing. In this way, various stages and variations can exist between the two opposed courses of aiming at the establishment of individuality and of living by setting up categories and boundaries; these differences in ways of thinking and viewing the individual undoubtedly constitute one set of stimuli for changes in language.

Men's language and women's language

The Japanese thinking about men and women is another clue to changes in the speaker. The Japanese language has different speech forms for men and women. Particular expressions used only by women are thought to demonstrate their gentleness, and criticism of women college students for talking like men often appears in the newspapers. This philosophy of there being a womanly and a manly way of talking, and the resulting distinctive speech forms, will, of course, change if there is any shift in what is expected of women and men in Japanese society.

Broadly speaking, the societal differences between men and women have been lessening somewhat in Japan recently, as can be seen in dress and outward behavior. In language as well, women's speech may be becoming somewhat more masculine, but at the same time a larger portion of men's speech is becoming more feminine. Of course, this leveling-out process is not following a uniform pattern; and in certain areas, clear-cut differences still exist in the language used toward and by men and women.

In present elementary, junior high, and senior high schools, women teachers attach *kun* to the names of boy students and *san* to the names of girl students; most boy students prefer *kun* and would be unhappy if addressed with *san*. Previously, the custom was for any female speaker to use *san* toward all students, male or female. In this case, the criterion for use has shifted from the speaker to the listener, but students have been adapting to the older style after graduating and going out into the wider society.

But we cannot conclude that this adaptation to the usage in society will continue indefinitely. The standards that now make such adaptation necessary may well change at some future time.

'Mottainai'

Considerable changes also seem to be taking place in how the Japanese view inanimate objects. For example, consider the phrase *mottainai* (It's wasteful). Both young people and older people frequently use this phrase, but there are clear differences in how they use it. For those in their forties or fifties or above, the major object of *mottainai* is food; and they are still influenced by the older, and now dying, way of thinking that considers throwing away even one grain of rice that has fallen to the floor wasteful. Young people, however, tend to use *mottainai* for the waste of labor or time.

Thinking of objects and human beings as having an indivisible relationship, as explained earlier in this book in regard to the sentence, *Sutoobu-o kowashite-shimatta* (I broke the heater), is a very common tendency in Japan; but thinking of objects in terms of themselves alone, and apart from their relationship with human beings, also seems to be quite strong at present. Recently, many students feel no resistance to praising, and thereby evaluating, their teacher's teaching methods or written works.

The view of animals also seems to be in the process of change. We cannot go so far as to say that the gap between the attitude toward dolphins and whales held by older Japanese and by young Japanese is as great as that between Japanese and Americans, but the diet of the Japanese is moving away from fish to meat, resulting in a weakening of the feeling of fish as a food. No one can say for sure that the Japanese image of sea mammals as being in the same family as fish will not change to their being in the category of mammals instead. And at that time, we may see accounts about how the Japanese of a generation before cruelly slaughtered those mammals.

Not just a linguistic matter

The way Japanese think about their language will, of course, have a large effect on the future of the Japanese language. Some Japanese now hold the view that words are essentially meaningless and only heart or feeling is important, while others have the older conception of Japanese as possessing a special spiritual power of its own. Many other attitudes toward language are also present. What will the Japanese of the future emerging out of this confused situation be like?

Considerable changes have also occurred in the views of language and language education, the ideas underlying debates about language education policy and methods. Some people believe that in Japan's increasingly internationalized society it is essential to know English, but others believe that the Japanese incline too much toward English and should instead study Chinese and Korean, the languages of its neighbors; the latter also advocate paying more attention to the other languages spoken by the three-billion people of the world. Still others think that the Japanese do not learn foreign languages well and that these are not so important for them: they should spend their time learning other subjects instead. Thus, many different views exist concerning language and language education, preventing the emergence of any general consensus regarding second-language education.

We have discussed the attitudes of the speaker toward human beings, objects, and language as factors which are deeply related to the use of language and influential in language change. Another important consideration is the individual's view of how one should live. At any rate, we have seen that linguistic problems are not a matter of words alone. Thus, when letters to the editor criticize the careless or disrespectful way of talking of workers in shops and small restaurants, it is clear that merely giving them language training will by no means constitute a fundamental solution to this problem. Similarly, if we wish to create a superior and appropriate Japanese, draw up ideal plans for language usage, or establish effective teaching methods, these must all be based on the recognition that these are not problems of words alone.

Consequently, in this chapter we have attempted to

pinpoint the problem through looking at the life style of the Japanese, a possible factor in language change, and at various elements in actual verbal communication — the content, environment, and means of communication, as well as the listener and speaker. I would like to stress here that the key to many problems in verbal communication actually lies in solving the problems of the speaker, those of human beings themselves.

EXPECTATIONS TOWARD LANGUAGE EDUCATION (1)

The Japanese language in an internationalized society

Before the late 19th century, it required over ten days to travel from Tokyo (then Edo) to Kyoto. Today it takes only a little over two hours and forty minutes by bullet train; indeed, by the latest nonstop route, it is only twelve hours from Tokyo to New York. This trip to the other side of the globe which required tens of days in the age of ships will probably be even shorter when supersonic passenger flights are introduced. All those living today have been affected in some way or other by this shrinking of the earth.

In this book, I have noted how the increase in contacts with strangers, i.e. with people not sharing the same ways of living and thinking, has inevitably led to language change. In the midst of these great changes, it is probably impossible to preserve as is the forms and ways of doing things from an earlier age; and if one attempts to do so, the problem is how to best adapt them to correspond to the new conditions present today.

Appropriate communication is necessary in order to develop and grow, to cope with urbanization within Japan, and to preserve an orderly societal life in the midst of internationalization. We must develop the language and language ability to make that possible.

In this age, the expectations placed on foreign-language education in order to cope with internationalization are heavy indeed, and teaching methods and materials strongly oriented to the introduction of foreign culture are no longer sufficient: one must instead aim at the ability to assert one's opinions in a foreign language. And that should not be biased toward the traditional languages of the advanced nations; the Japanese should stop overlooking the languages of the developing world. It is time to throw off such near-sighted policies as those in which economic problems, such as the oil shock, are the starting point for cultural exchange and foreign-language policy.

Further, the idea that interchange with a foreign country is only possible in that country's language is now out of date. If the Japanese desire exchange on an equal footing and under conditions for the mutual benefit of both parties, they must take steps to open up exchange in Japanese. For if language is culture, then the expression of the thinking and emotions of the Japanese in foreign languages alone cannot help but be inadequate.

The number of foreigners studying Japanese has increased dramatically in recent years. The motives of these some 300,000 Japanese-language students are all different, but they share the common desire to learn about Japan and gain an understanding of Japanese culture. Their studying Japanese is evidence that they wanted something more from Japan than technology or natural science in English, and felt the limitations of acquiring that knowledge through English or other foreign languages.

An age has arrived in which we should no longer allow Japanese language and culture to remain confined to Japan.

The development of independent, active human beings

I stated above that the development of new means of communication and spread of automation have given rise to a life without speech and without written characters. The advent of television may have lessened still further the time spent in talking, an area traditionally little valued and relatively passive in Japan. If such practices as watching television together with one's guests rather than conversing with them, or of young people on a date finding it hard to talk to each other and using a television computer game as intermediary instead, become deeply rooted among the Japanese, we cannot hope for the development of a people who can cope with internationalization.

Television is a representative case of how the development of civilization can tend to make people more passive. Yet there has been little recognition of how important the cultivation of human beings who can respond positively and actively to these changes in the life environment is for the future of Japan, indeed for the future of the human race. Strong interest exists in creating and operating the most efficient facilities and machinery, but efforts to help humans make the most of such an environment are lagging far behind the speed of change. We must develop independent and active individuals capable of coping with a physical environment changing at a dizzying rate. Moreover, that capacity should not be limited to a small elite but should be given to all the people; in order to do so, this must not stop at the abstract stage of classroom knowledge and ability, but must be the springboard for concrete actions and knowledge in everyday life. And the individual's abilities and knowledge to deal with society must be thought of in terms of the individual; respect for the individual is not something to be grasped simply in the context of one's relative relations with others.

EXPECTATIONS TOWARD LANGUAGE EDUCATION (2)

Toward an education in everyday spoken Japanese

If Japanese college students are asked to write the tables of the *hiragana* and *katakana* syllabaries, a considerable number of them cannot do so completely and in the correct order. Their *katakana* シ (shi) and ツ (tsu), ン (n) and ソ (so), are hard to tell apart, as are their *hiragana* そ (so) and ろ (ro). Mistakes in the order include placing wa and (w)o before ra, ri, ru, re, ro and putting ya, yu, yo, wa, (w)o together in one line instead of on separate lines.

The same students, however, can give the ABC alphabet from beginning to end without any mistakes. Both the Japanese a-i-u-e-o and the ABC alphabet are used to order the entries in dictionaries and the like throughout daily life. What is the meaning of Japanese students being able to give the foreign ABC alphabet but not the Japanese a-i-u-e-o one?

This problem is not found in Japan alone; the declining ability of young students in their own language is being commented on in the United States and the countries of Europe as well. That phenomenon may be an inevitable result of world internationalization, and a case might even be made for its desirability; on the other hand, it can also be viewed as a loss of self that comes from moving along unthinkingly under the stimulus of foreign culture.

It is a fact that today's youth in Japan is far behind older people in the ability to read and write, with many not being able to write a letter satisfactorily. But this does not necessarily mean that today's youth as a group is inferior in language skills to the youth of thirty years ago.

As far as speaking ability is concerned, we must plainly acknowledge the superiority of today's youth. The youth of a generation ago and today's older Japanese cannot come close to them in the ability to express their thoughts and emotions. One cause of this is probably the changes in means of communication and the shift from a writing-oriented to a speaking-oriented life, and another large influence has been the postwar educational system and social climate respecting the expression of individuality.

However, we must hesitate before therefore concluding that the speaking skills of youth today leave nothing whatsoever to be desired. Verbal communication is first accomplished when the speaker's message is conveyed to a listener. Only through the use of language based on a shared understanding is it possible to overcome the distance between two persons. Even though young people can enjoy a lively talk with friends in a coffee shop, it seems that they cannot make an orderly presentation of some matter in a more formal situation; we must therefore judge them to be lacking in the language skills of responsible adults in Japanese society.

As I have pointed out before, language is not the sole property of any one person, but the common property of the whole society. Since anything unintelligible to the listener is no longer language, primary importance must be given to reflecting on one's own language behavior in order to achieve the most effective communication possible.

However, it is by no means a simple matter to reflect on one's own language skills. Not only young people but all Japanese have few opportunities to take a fresh look at Japanese. The questions of foreigners studying Japanese provide one such opportunity. For example, why do some Japanese say *itsutsu kudasai* (five, please) and others *itsutsu-gurai* or *itsutsu-hodo* (about five) when buying five apples, as discussed earlier? Or why do people you meet in the street in your neighborhood always seem to intrusively ask, *Dochira-e odekake-desu-ka* (literally, Where are you going?)? Most Japanese will probably not be able to give clear answers if asked these questions by foreigners. In fact, many foreigners are irritated by this question *Dochira-e odekake-desu-ka* because they regard it as a real question, rather than as the greeting that most Japanese mean it to be. To continue, what is the difference between *Soo-desu-ne* (That's so) and *Soo-desu-yo* (That's so!)? Are *hai* (yes) and "yes" the same? Endless examples can be given of common expressions like these which one uses unthinkingly in daily life, but would be hard pressed to explain if asked about their meaning.

Most discussions about pronunciation and way of talking in Japan seem to end in simply criticizing accents or ways of talking different from one's own, with no objective pointing out of the facts of the matter. And we can say that not being able to correctly write the fifty-sounds table of the *hiragana* and *katakana* syllabaries indicates how much interest most Japanese have in the sound system of Japanese.

The above evidence lends support to the thesis that the Japanese largely take the spoken language for granted, regarding it as something overly familiar and of little value, and feeling that they know everything there is to know about it.

What kind of education would serve to further reflection on the language used in actual life? It is fair to say that language education in Japanese schools now leans toward works of literature and difficult expository writings and neglects education in the contemporary language. Training in composition is conducted, and chances to polish one's written power of expression are provided; but it is questionable how useful that is as systematic training in the spoken language, the language used in one's everyday life.

In addition, although roughly half of the time in English classes in Japanese schools is actually spent in speaking or writing in Japanese, these are regarded as classes in English alone, and no attention is paid to the Japanese used. No problem is made of strange sentences literally translated from English as long as they convey the meaning of the English sentences, no matter how remote they are from the language used in everyday life.

I am not questioning the value of coming into contact with outstanding Japanese literary works or learning a foreign language. However, how can one understand such literary works if one does not have a basic grasp of the everyday language? How can one understand and be able to use a foreign language if one cannot use one's own language well?

I believe that no fundamental solution of the various problems of language study in Japan is possible as long as the values sought after remain outside the learning process, and no new appreciation of the values within the learning process itself takes place. If the Japanese do not value the everyday spoken language, and are not given systematic and logical training in its conscious use, then all efforts to protect the beauty of the Japanese language and to master foreign languages will be in vain.

References

1. Shiraishi Daiji: *Kaisetsu Hyoojungo Jiten*, Asakura Shoten, 1962.
   白石大二「解説標準語事典」（朝倉書店、昭和37年）

2. Waseda University Institute of Language Teaching: *Chuugokugo to Taioo-suru Kango*, Agency for Cultural Affairs, 1978.
   早稲田大学語学教育研究所「中国語と対応する漢語」（文化庁、昭和53年）

3. *Yomiuri Shimbun*, April 1977.
   「読売新聞」（昭和52年4月）

INDEX

Advantage and disadvantage, concern with, 112-115
Aizuchi, 81-86
Arbitrariness, of language, 152-53
Are, 49-51, 99-101
Automation, influence of, 146-48
Boku, 105
Change, attitude toward, 102-3
Complaining, 62, 73-74
Consideration toward others, 31-32, 90, 95-99, 150-51
Debate, attitude toward, 71-72
Deletion, of understood words: *Ocha-o doozo*, 24; *Densha-ga okureta . . .*, 35-37; *Uchi ni kaettara . . .*, 37-38; *Kyooto-e ikimashita*, 45-48; *Biiru . . .*, 48-49; *Kaettara denwa-shimasu*, 160; *Yoroshikattara . . .*, 161
Denial, 91-95, 118
Emotion, expression of, 76-77
English, influence of, 142-44
Equality. See Inequality, dislike of

Evaluation, attitude toward, 110-11, 125, 168
Factual, stress on, 154-57
Foreign-language education, in Japan, 27, 169, 171
Foreigners, attitude toward, 16-17, 63-67
"Friend", 130
Greetings, 13-17, 58-61, 151, 163
Group consciousness, 61-63, 87, 130-35
Gurai, 88-90, 158-59
Hai, 82-85
"He said he went", 154-55
Higher-lower distinction, 121-27, 138-40, 165
Hodo, 88-90, 158-59
"How much is this?", answer to, 25, 98-99
Ichioo, 93-95
Iie, 91-93
Indirect form of expression: *samui-nee*, 31-32; *ichioo*, 93-95; *are*, 99-101; *kashira*, 137-38
Inequality, dislike of, 109-10, 139-40
Insider-outsider distinction, 58, 61-62, 127-33, 165-66. See also Foreigners, attitude toward

Intonation, 33-36, 63, 83-84
Jippon, 20-21
Joint production, of conversation, 83-88
Keredomo, 161-62
Kinship terms, use of, 104-6, 122-23, 127
Konnichi-wa, 13-17
Kore, sore, are, dore, 49-51. See also *Are, Sore*
Kowaremashita, 117-118
Kowashimashita, 117-18
Language, humble, 91-92, 119-23
Language, men's, 166-67
Language, polite, 126
Language, respect, 122-23, 126-27, 157
Language, women's, 137-38, 166-67
Logical expression, 74-76, 161-62
The Magnificent Seven, 67-68
Meetings, Japanese, 56, 71-73, 103
Mottainai, 167-68
Nonverbal communication: pointing, 39-40; physical distance, 40-41; facial expression, 42-43; bowing, 41, 44; *haragei*, 53
Nuclear family, influence of, 149-51
Ocha-o doozo, 24
Ohayoo gozaimasu, 13-15

Okaasan, extended use of, 104-5
Omoiyari, 32, 90, 95-99, 150-51
Order of speaking, 56-57
Ordering (food), 134-35
Orders, attitude toward, 136-38
Osekkai, 96-98
Passive, 113-14, 143
Persuasion, attitude toward, 69-70
Praise, attitude toward, 119-20, 125-26, 168
Prominence (of sound), 35-36
Pronunciation, attitude toward, 19-24
Recommendation, letters of, 110-11
Refusal, 92-95
Responsibility, attitude toward, 117-19
San, 128-29, 167
Sayoonara, 124
Senjitsu-wa doomo, 102
Senpai, and *koohai*, 129
Sensee, 123-24, 128-29
The Seven Samurai, 67-68
Shikashi, 161-62
Signs, change in, 157-58
Silence, attitude toward, 53-55, 57, 73, 159
Situation, dependence on, 24, 35-38, 47-49, 160-62
Soo-desu-ne, 33-34, 96
Sore, 49-50, 100-101

179

Speeches, fondness of, 55-56
Standardization, of Japanese, 144-46
Status, vs identity, 107
Telephone, conversation on, 83-84
Tennis, English as, 86-87
Tomodachi, 130
Volleyball, Japanese as, 86-88
Words, life without, 146-48
Words, low expectations of, 75-78
Writing, attitude toward, 18-22
Writing, decline in, 148-49
"Yes", 82-83, 85
Young people, language of, 63, 163-64, 173-74